They Saw Jesus

Modern Day Face to Face Encounters with Jesus Christ

David Holdaway

Life Publications

Acknowledgements

I would like to thank all those whose stories and testimonies of seeing Jesus are mentioned in this book. A big thank you to those who have prayed for me in the writing of this book. A special thank you to Cathy Carter for helping to review the manuscript and my wife Jan, as always, has been an invaluable help in editing and proof-reading the text.

Revised and updated 2012

Revised 2020

E–mail: davidholdaway1@aol.com

ISBN 978-0-9554594-2-9

www.lifepublications.org.uk

"Let me see Thy face even if I die,
lest I die with longing to see it!"

Augustine, Confessions I.V

Dedicated

To

Ronald Holdaway

My beloved father who went to be with Jesus the week before I completed this book.

Now he is seeing Him face to face.

Contents

Direction and Deliverance Encounters

Group Encounters

Encounters Beyond The Veil

Appendices

Introduction

Dr John White is a psychiatrist and former missionary in Latin America who has a worldwide speaking and writing ministry. He was the associate professor of psychiatry at the University of Manitoba for many years. He has written numerous books, including *Eros Defiled*, *The Golden Cow*, *When the Spirit Comes with Power* and many others.

He says that on one occasion as he prayed with some friends, he saw the arms and hands of Christ extended towards him. He said that his eyes were open, that he was fully aware of his surroundings and that his experience was in three dimensions and full colour and the effect was overwhelming.

"All strength left me, so that it was with difficulty that I remained kneeling. I began to sweat profusely and tremble uncontrollably," he recalled.

He also speaks of another encounter that he had while in Honolulu in the summer of 1990.

"I was sitting on a settee, and was wondering what it would be like to have Jesus sitting next to me. Jesus was suddenly there, sitting at the other end of the settee, although I could see Jesus only in outline, and could see through Him. Jesus sat there for a moment, and then raised His arm and placed His hand on my left hand that rested on the back of the settee. After a while Jesus stood up to go, and I said, 'Please don't go, stay.' While Jesus sat there on the settee, I was unable to see His eyes, but when Jesus got up to leave I saw them."

He described the experience as one in which he felt that he was "penetrating into the beyond." [1]

I have a very good friend in Aberdeen, Scotland, who has been a follower of Jesus for more than 75 years. His life was dramatically changed when as a teenager he was seriously ill in hospital and one night he saw Jesus at the foot of his bed. He said he knew then that he would make a full recovery. Today as I write he has just celebrated his 89th birthday and the doctors said his latest medical showed he was A1.

These are just a couple of the dozens of accounts detailed in this book of those who have had "face to face" encounters with Jesus. Some like Dr John White are well known leaders others like my friend are relatively unknown but the encounter has been equally real and life changing.

The criteria I have used to include and assess such encounters have been:

i). They have a biblical framework and are consistent with Scripture.

ii). Something significant took place because of the encounter which acts as another source of verification such as a miracle, healing, supernatural impartation of knowledge etc.

iii). The person or persons involved in the encounter exhibit the character and ministry that help to substantiate what they have said.

Such vision and apparition experiences in which people believe they encounter Jesus Christ have been reported among Christians for two thousand years. This should not surprise us because Jesus rose from the dead and is alive. As I have researched this book I have come across hundreds of such Christic encounters and what is interesting is that there are so few similar experiences claimed for the leaders of other religions. Indeed, as you will read those from such faiths were crying out for God and it was not Mohammed or Krishna or Buddha who appeared but Jesus Christ. This should not surprise us either because they did not rise from death, they are dead. While many religious leaders rose to greatness only Jesus rose from the grave.

I am well aware that there is much confusion and counterfeit when it comes to investigating such experiences and encounters. There is also a great deal of the weird and the wacky. Therefore I have been careful in using the above criteria in evaluating the accounts mentioned in this book. I do not claim that each one is inerrant but we need to realise that if there is a counterfeit it is only because there is also the real thing.

I am also aware of Jesus' words, *"Blessed are those who have not seen and yet have believed,"* (John 20:29) . The Bible is all the proof anyone needs that Jesus is alive and that He is Lord. He is *"the same yesterday, today and forever,"* (Hebrews 13:8).

There are also a number of appendices at the back which deal with theological and historical issues in more detail. I have had to limit the material because of the size of the book but they should be sufficient to stimulate and help you regarding further study.

I have been blessed beyond measure writing this book, I pray that you will be equally blessed reading it and if you don't yet know the living Jesus as your Lord and Saviour you will do so before you get to the end. May the following pages change your life forever.

David Holdaway

Salvation Encounters

1

FRED LEMON

Breakout

"It was very quiet in my cell after the warder had escorted me back from the 'dungeons' – the punishment cells – and locked me in for the night. Distant sounds reached me; the clanging of other doors, a heavy trolley being moved, a man shouting on another landing.

"I took no notice. After a day in the dungeons a man's mind can be possessed by an overwhelming despair. Back here in my cell an atmosphere of evil seemed still to be with me; in memory I read again the plea of some long ago prisoner, carved roughly on the cold, gray walls, 'My God, my God, why hast thou forsaken me?'

"If there had been room in my heart for pity I might have spared some for that unknown man. Forsaken – yes, that summed it up alright.

"I threw myself on the hard bed, a black bitterness of soul filling me. Tomorrow, I vowed, I would get hold of the sharpest knife in the mailbag room – and there would be murder done. We would see then whether God cared or not...Weary and tormented I pulled the coarse blanket round my shoulders and closed my eyes.

"Something made me sit up suddenly. There were three men in the cell with me; they were dressed in ordinary civvy suits. The man on the right spoke, 'Fred,' he said, 'This is Jesus...'"

So reads the introduction to Fred Lemon's amazing story in his book *Breakout*.

Born at the beginning of the First World War Fred was placed in a home with his brother when he was just five years old. Eight years later he found himself in a remand home and then to Hertfordshire Training School at Ware, the youngest boy ever to be sent there. The pattern of crime and punishment, bravado and misery had begun.

Fred became a vicious criminal, greedy, devious and violent and an habitual burglar. Although he was involved in many robberies and was a top police suspect, they never seemed to have the proof they needed to convict him, so he became rather complacent. Eventually, after being caught in possession of stolen goods, he was arrested and appeared at the Old Bailey. Fred was filled with self confidence and reckoned he could talk his way out of this little lot without too much trouble. He said, "The judge had eyed me with clear, blue eyes, the trusting, open eyes of a kindly old gentleman. But when he began to pronounce sentence, those eyes became steel hard, his voice like ice splinters – 'You will go to prison for two years...' It was April 1945 and he served his time in Wormwood Scrubs, where his one ambition was to become a bigger and better thief. When he came out he was a hardened criminal who armed himself with a gun and was he said, "ready for anything."

Convinced that his wife, Doris, had shopped him to the police his hatred and resentment for her grew until twice while drunk he tried to strangle her. He had his hands around her throat squeezing the life out of her but each time something held him back.

After almost killing a man during a robbery Fred was sentenced to another five years in prison. Two prison officers had to grab him as he tried to leap over the dock. Shouting and swearing he was dragged off to the prison van and driven to Wandsworth Jail. There he was violent and uncooperative and pretty soon he was summoned to the Governor's office and told, "You are a trouble maker of the worst kind. You will be transferred to Dartmoor Prison."

Dartmoor had a reputation as one of the worst prisons in the country. Fred was told, "Only the scum go there." There would be unremitting hard labour and punishment cells where a man could go mad.

Fred was given a cell that was worse than most, situated next to the latrine recess which made the air damp and foul. His room measured just nine feet long by six foot wide with a grey stone floor and just one tiny window. Here he was to spend the next five years of his life. It didn't take long before he hated everything about his new surroundings and especially some of the warders whom he detested, and they did everything they could to make his life even more of a misery.

Over the long tedious months Fred hatched a plan to escape but to do so he needed to get a fellow inmate to make a diversion and the best way of making contact with him was to join the Methodist service on Sundays which his mate also attended. Little did he realise how much his life was about to change as that Sunday morning, the chaplain, Rev Percy Holmes, spoke to the men about the love of God and that peace and happiness were a free gift of God; all you had to do was to take it, through Jesus. Fred never forgot that moment; it was September 3, 1949, his thirty-fifth birthday.

Abandoning his escape plans, Fred spoke to the chaplain personally and began to read his Bible much to the scorn of his fellow-prisoners. Things in his life began to change yet his old ways still had a hold on him, especially his violent temper and insolence to some of the guards. Rejected by many of his former mates and ridiculed and mocked mercilessly by some of the officers Fred found himself in the punishment cells on a charge set up by one of his guards. The punishment was just to sit there, alone in your bleak, bitterly cold cell with no furniture or books, other than a Bible, all day long for as many days as you were sentenced. Usually it meant going on a number one diet, bread and water for three days, then back to ordinary food for three days and so on to bread and water again. It also meant a loss of privileges when you finally left there.

Fred felt that everything was against him and even though he still forced himself to read a chapter of the Bible each day he no longer found the strength and peace in it he once had. Instead he was being consumed with anger because of the injustice he had been suffering. He decided that the next screw (officer) to put him on a charge would get 'a knife in his guts.' He hadn't long to wait. He was at the centre of an outburst in the mailbag room and found himself in the dungeons again. There he nursed his wrath against the warders and relived their insults and victimisations. Christianity just wasn't worth it, he told himself, "The only thing that paid off in this world was being tough and holding your own against people in authority. You had to stand up for yourself."

Embittered and depressed beyond measure he returned to his cell obsessed with a plan for the following day to knife the guard who had most made his life a torment. Fred says, "The Bible was where I had left it on the shelf. For a moment I looked at its cover, hesitating. Then I shrugged and turned away. What did it all matter? Who would grieve for me apart from my wife Doris, if I got hanged for killing a guard?" Wearily he crawled under the blanket and closed his eyes.

That night, August 10th, 1950, Fred woke up to find three men standing in his cell. They wore ordinary – though immaculate civilian suits; that much he could clearly see, though their faces seemed shaded in some way. He swung his legs out of bed and sat bold upright on the edge, wide awake. He describes what happened next:

"The man on the right spoke my name. Fred, 'This is Jesus' he said. The middle figure, at whom he pointed, began to talk to me. Gently, clearly, he traced my whole life up to this desperate day. The lies, the pilfering, the eager thrusting into worse and worse adventures in crime, the few efforts to show a kindness and the heartless attacks I had made on my gentle wife... and now, after all the new hope, peace and joy of my ventures into faith, the precipice-edge on which I now stood poised...

"I listened to every word, my head resting on my hands as I sat there on my bed. Strangely, I felt no sense of fear, or even awe, and all the remorse about my past was wiped out by a warm certainty that through this Jesus, God was offering me forgiveness – had already, in fact, forgiven all my sin.

"I can remember no words of that wonderful talk in detail, except the last sentence which the Lord Jesus spoke. 'If you want to become a Christian, you must drive the hatred from your heart.' I knew He spoke the truth, and I knew He referred to my attitude to the warders.

"As those words were spoken I raised my head and looked up. The three figures, still facing me, were fading through the wall. There was a distinct 'click' – and I was alone.

"'That was Jesus Himself,' I said aloud, 'The Lord Jesus Christ has been here, in this cell.' There was no fear, no terror of the mysterious unknown. A great peace took possession of me, and I lay back on the bed, to sleep like a child, dreamless and unafraid."

In the morning Fred knew it had been no dream but became afraid and confused wondering what it all meant. He thought he might have been going mad and seeing things. All sorts of strange things happened in men's minds when they had been kept in solitary confinement. Who would believe him? He decided to tell no one except the chaplain Percy Holmes when he retuned.

He tried to act as normal as possible but was in a kind of daze. Part of him clinging to the wonder and joy and peace which he had known in Jesus' presence and another part reaching out to rekindle the hatred to attack his enemies. A terrible battle was raging within.

In that state of turmoil he made his way to the mailbag room where the most hated guard, Tojo, was in charge. Fred found himself staring at him convinced he was the reason for all his troubles. If he was out of the way it would be easy to be a Christian – it was he who was keeping alive the evil in his nature.

Faint and far away Fred heard again Jesus' words, "You must drive the evil from your heart." But they were drowned out by the anger filled voice of Tojo barking out his orders to the men. The devil driving him, Fred picked up a knife staring wildly at the man he hated and the atmosphere became charged with evil. As the guard came closer Fred's hand tightened on the handle of the knife but his arm had gone completely numb, all power had left it and he couldn't lift it an inch, it was completely paralysed. As Tojo moved away, strength gradually came back into his arm and he put his knife down.

Fred was sweating, he had never known anything like this, he knew it was God who had held back his arm from committing that terrible deed. Shame and gratitude surged through him and the head he bent over his work that morning was a head bent in prayer. Again God had miraculously intervened.

These two events were a major turning point. Fred began to pray for the guards he had once hated and the prison Governor told him he could see a great change in his life and promoted him to the top job in the prison for an inmate, as the Governor's orderly. The guards reported that the old anger and rage had gone and Fred had a new look of love and peace in his eyes.

When he left jail he knew he would never return. His life had changed forever. He became a Christian preacher and evangelist, speaking at many churches, and youth events, and visiting prisons to testify how Jesus Christ had met with him and changed his life. He set up an open, caring home with his wife Doris and they adopted five needy children. He became a greengrocer by profession and a powerful, passionate evangelist by persuasion.

Reflecting many years later on the events of that momentous night and the following morning, Fred admitted he didn't know why Jesus had chosen to appear to him or why after such an encounter he still had murder in his heart. But he was overawed and overwhelmed by God's grace reaching out to such as him.

2

DOREEN IRVING

From Witchcraft to Christ

When I first read Doreen Irving's book *From Witchcraft to Christ* I found it utterly compelling and totally believable. During the twenty five years since then my own personal experiences of helping people be set free from witchcraft and the occult have confirmed many times how dark and destructive such things are and how wonderful and all powerful Jesus is.

As queen of the black witches, Doreen Irving was involved and mired in witchcraft as much as anyone could be. Her lifestyle as a drug addict, strip tease artist and prostitute had only made her involvement in satanism and witchcraft easier as she looked for power, pleasure and prestige wherever she could find it.

She tells of her terrifying encounter when she saw her "master," Satan, at the foot of her bed threatening her to have nothing to do with Jesus or Christianity. She also shares how on two separate occasions she also saw Jesus who had come to heal her and set her free.

Her story

"Two girls were standing together in the semi-darkness of the strip club, whispering in hushed voices. I had noticed them before, a strange bond held them together and there was something eerie about them and I decided to investigate. I crept up behind them and heard them whispering something about the satanists' temple. I wanted to know more so I stepped out of the shadows and said brightly, "What's all this about the satanists' temples?" The two girls were startled and said they couldn't tell me anything as it was a secret. They must have thought I had overheard the entire conversation so agreed to tell me more provided I promised never to divulge a word of it to anyone. They said they were satanists and worshipped at the temple of Satan. I wanted to go too and so the next night at 6pm sharp I got into a large black car with them and was instructed by the driver to put on a blindfold. The journey was over in no time and when the blindfold was removed what I saw was astonishing and very mysterious. I was in a very large hall with about 500 people. A platform at the front was draped in black and on a throne like seat sat a robed and hooded figure. His garments were embroidered with snakes, dragons and flames of fire. Around him in a semi circle stood some thirteen figures, also robed in black.

"A satanist ceremony unfolded during which the chief satanist came over to me and asked if I wanted to join. He said he hoped to see me again. I wasn't sure if I would go again but some power drew me back to the next meeting where I witnessed all manner of evil scenes. I was more than a little flattered when the chief satanist asked me to join him for a meal and he seemed to know all about me. He told me that all kinds of people were satanists, from the high to the low – bankers, shopkeepers, teachers, nurses, prostitutes, drug addicts. He said there was no difference between them as their aim was to promote Satan on the earth whenever and however they could. He had a strong personality and had no difficultly in persuading me to become a satanist. My friendship with him grew and I attended all the meetings and I was eager to become a full fledged satanist. I learned that satanism twisted and distorted everything, a lie was in fact the truth, it was a kind of brain washing.

“The chief satanist became a regular visitor to the strip club where I still worked bringing me a constant supply of heroin for which he would accept no payment. I was now his mistress. One day he informed me that I was ready to become a sworn in child of Lucifer. I was dressed in a black robe at an elaborate ceremony with almost a thousand present. Hymns and prayers were made to the god of darkness, death and mystery. During the ritual the chief satanist approached me and made an incision in my left arm, and my blood was caught in the cup that contained blood from a slain bird. The knife was kissed and the blood mixed. I then drank some of this blood and made my vows to Satan. Next I dipped my finger into the mixed blood and signed a real parchment, thereby selling my soul to Satan for ever and ever, to be his slave for all eternity. I was now a true satanist and the people went crazy, and all kinds of evil scenes followed with much wickedness being done that evening. To my surprise I was sworn in as a high priestess, a great honour and when I protested that I wasn’t ready for such distinction, the chief satanist said it was a request of Lucifer himself, and he must be obeyed. Satan was now my master. I even heard his audible voice and saw him materialise in front of me.

“As the months went by my knowledge of evil grew. I needed very little sleep and I was given supernatural strength. I was truly a slave of Satan and keeping my vows well. One day, I was having a drink with my lover and master, the chief satanist, when he informed me he was also a black witch who practiced black magic. Witchcraft of the black kind is not far removed from satanism. The main difference between the two is that satanists worship the devil in the satanist temple, whereas witches attend a coven of thirteen witches, one of whom is their head. They require no temple. Witchcraft can be practiced anywhere but preferably in a quiet, remote setting, such as a deserted house, a lonely beach or a wood. The witching hour of midnight is also preferred, and activities are conducted by moonlight. "Warlock" is the correct name for a person usually called a witch. Black witches have great power and are able to call up or call down powers of darkness to help them. They hold nothing sacred and will stop at nothing to pursue their goals. Black witches and satanists believe that in the ultimate battle between good and evil, evil will triumph. They believe that Lucifer will one day conquer Christ and will retrieve what they call his rightful place. Satan, they affirm, will rule the earth, sea and heavens. Hell, for a witch of the black kind, is not a place of torment but of unlimited pleasure, with every lust fulfilled. Be warned: those who walk down the dark road of witchcraft lose their reason, often going completely insane. God is called evil, which does not make sense. Minds are twisted and warped.

"The chief satanist encouraged me to become a black witch, his dark eyes flashing as he spoke almost hypnotising me. His face shone with a strange, eerie light I'd never seen before. It can be no worse that satanism I reasoned. I had witnessed evil and ugly orgies in the satanists' temple, but I was to see far worse in the witches' coven. At my initiation goat's blood was smeared all over my naked body. Things followed that were too evil to be brought to mind.

"My powers as a black witch were great, and I added to my knowledge of evil every day. My ability to levitate four or five feet was very real. Demons aided me. Killing birds in flight after they had been let loose from a cage was another act I performed as a witch. I could also make objects disappear. I practiced more wickedness in a single week than many would in a lifetime. My name was submitted by the chief Satanist to become queen of the black witches. The test of my power was held on Dartmoor in Devon. I exhibited my powers in a remarkable way one moonlit night.

"A great ceremony was held a short time after at which the next queen of black witches was to be chosen. Black witches from all parts of England assembled, as well as witches from Holland, Germany and France. They arrived before Halloween, when Dartmoor was a hive of activity. The ceremony commenced with chants to ancient gods and demons and after the rituals the great test of power began. Seven witches including me were competing for the title. A bird was released from a cage which I killed in flight. Then came the final test – fire walking.

"The test was to walk through a great bonfire. The successful candidate would meet Lucifer in the centre of the blaze and Lucifer would be seen to take the hand of the witch and guide her through the flames so that she would emerge completely unscathed. I walked confidently into the flames of seven feet or more, all the time calling on my great master, Diablos. Suddenly I saw him materialise before me – a great black figure. I took his hand and walked with him to the centre of the great blaze. There, I paused, the great flames leaping around me.

"Only when I emerged at the other side of the blaze did my master Diablos disappear. Not even the smell of burning was upon my loose witch's robe or my long flowing hair. Everyone was prostrated on the ground, chanting, 'Hail, Diana, queen of black witches!' It was the cry of over a thousand witches. A crown of pure gold was placed on my head and a cloak embroidered with gold draped around my shoulders and an orb of gold placed in my left hand. I took my seat on the throne which had been prepared before the ceremony. Wild and frenzied celebrations followed.

"As queen of the black witches I was held in great esteem and travelled in luxury with the chief satanist all over Europe. We held many discussions with other high ranking witches and satanists on how to make witchcraft more appealing as many people, especially the young, were taking a fresh interest in the occult. We outlined our plan as guidelines were laid down. Never frighten anyone. Make witchcraft less sinister. Make it look like natural innocent adventure. New recruits were needed if evil was to conquer. Now was the time to trap people. Once people were involved in witchcraft it would be too late for them to get out. We witches were very devout in our cause and our discussions went on for hours on end.

"I was queen of black witches for a full year. Then I willingly stepped down to allow someone younger to take the title although I could have kept it if I wished. As soon as I gave up the title the chief satanist found a new mistress. I was hurt and angry but he was the chief satanist and no one questioned him. I left London and drifted from town to village for a few years, visiting London now and then to obtain drugs or worship at the temple of Satan. Life was a little less hectic but still as dark as the grave. These were unsettling years for me. I had one mounting fear – the fear of growing old and dying. As the fear grew, so questions arose in my mind. Was hell the wonderful place I had been led to believe? When the doubts persisted I decided to try and break away from witchcraft and satanism and even to visit a few Christian churches, just to see if they had the answer. Not that these visits were frequent, far from it, but the fact remains I at least went, something a black witch would never do. Always the fear of being found out haunted me, I constantly looked over my shoulder to make sure I wasn't being followed.

"Eventually after many roamings I moved to Bristol. I was back on the streets as a prostitute and hopelessly addicted to drugs but my feelings of loneliness and uncertainty grew. One summer evening I was out as usual on the familiar streets.

Two of my friends, also prostitutes, were with me. I suddenly stopped at the sight of a poster outside a church, it proclaimed in large bold letters *"Blessed are the pure in heart, for they shall see God."* It affected me greatly, anger and resentment swept over me as my sense of impurity overwhelmed me. I tore the poster down.

"Some months later I was out walking again, this time in the centre of Bristol. It was Monday morning and I noticed posters displayed in prominent places advertising a man called Eric Hutchings at the Colston Hall. At first I thought he was an "all in wrestler" and then found out he was an evangelist. I was so mad I pulled down every poster I could find.

"It was a lovely summer evening in June 1964. Three weeks had passed since I ripped down the posters and I had forgotten all about it. I was out on the streets plying my trade as a prostitute, high on drugs and drink when I noticed crowds of people all heading in one direction. Curious as ever I followed them and found myself at the Colston Hall. I was not in a good mood and had only one thing on my mind, to punch Eric Hutchings on the nose. I was shown to an empty seat at the end of a packed row and there I sat in low-cut black satin dress, my face heavily made up flaunting an assortment of jangling jewellery.

"The meeting began with a rousing hymn and I did not join in the singing but was looking for an exit. When the last hymn ended, everyone sat down – everyone except me, for I saw my chance to beat a hasty retreat. At that precise moment a hush fell on the large congregation as a woman with a sweet voice broke into song, filling the air with lovely music. It caused me to pause and listen:

> *I would love to tell you what I think of Jesus*
> *Since I found in Him a friend so strong and*
> *true.*
> *I would tell you how He changed my life completely,*
> *He's done something that no other friend could do.*

All my life was full of sin, when Jesus found me,
All my life was full of misery and woe.
Jesus placed His strong and loving arms around me,
And led me in the way I ought to go.

No one ever cared for me like Jesus.
There's no other friend so kind as He.
No one else could take the sin and darkness from me.
Oh! How much He cares for me.

"Something wonderful yet inexplicable was happening deep down inside me – something I'd never experienced before. My whole life unfolded before me as if projected on a screen. My mind was very clear, and I instantly sobered up. I saw myself as a child in Sunday School class and heard the teacher say, 'Why not let Jesus come into your heart?' I also saw the beds of shame and myself in the witches' covens. The realisation dawned on my black and sinful heart that no one really loved me – not the men on the streets or the men in the public houses, nor the satanists or the witches. Yet the singer said that Jesus cared and that Jesus could take the sin and awful darkness away. Could it really be true that this Jesus really lived and really cared? Could He care for me, a common prostitute, drug addict, and a witch? If it were true, I would surely love Him in return. How could I have missed such blessings all these long years? For the first time in my life I felt dirty and really ashamed of the life I'd lived.

"I had completely forgotten I was still standing up in the large hall. I was so sorry when the solo ended. I wished there had been fifty verses. I sat down subdued and shaken. The evangelist began his sermon, 'If you do not know the Lord Jesus Christ as your personal Saviour, you are lost, you are dead in trespasses and sins. The Bible says you are *bound*!' I jumped to my feet and shouted, 'he's right I am bound!' A shocked silence fell on the vast congregation, not to mention the preacher himself, when he continued he said that Jesus died for the who-so-ever and if they turn to Him He will set them free from the bondage of satan. My heart was beating very fast. Could He set me free? I remember no more of that powerful sermon. At the close the evangelist made an appeal, 'Come to Jesus tonight, come to the front.' People began going forward. Chains seemed to bind me to my seat as I heard the audible voice of Diablos, 'You are mine. You cannot go. It's too late for you. You are *MINE*.'

"I was shaking from head to foot. A great battle was going on inside me, a battle with the powers of darkness and satan. My evil master was fighting to hold on to me. The choir sang a second verse of *Just as I am*.

> *Just as I am, though tossed about*
> *With many a conflict, many a doubt,*
> *Fighting and fears within, without,*
> *Oh, Lamb of God, I come, I come!*

"By some tremendous miracle I was on my feet making my way to the front, Satan was losing the battle, Satan was losing his slave. Jesus who cared for me, even in all my sin and shame was tenderly wooing and winning my black and sinful heart. I was now standing at the front with tears falling down my painted face. 'I'm coming Jesus', I said softly. 'Please take this darkness away.' The Saviour heard my cry and accepted me *Just as I am*.

"I was not easy to counsel in the counselling room. My doubts and fears came flooding back in that changed atmosphere and I heard the voice of Satan say, 'You cannot change. You are *MINE*.' A great struggle was going on within. How could I live without drugs? What about my way of life? Several people spoke to me and I was given a copy of *St John's Gospel* with a little book called *First Steps with Christ*. As I left the hall a group of prostitutes were standing on the corner near by and they shouted to me and said they had been looking for me. I told them I had just got saved. They thought I was having a joke and laughed. I told them again that I had given my heart to Jesus and I was not joking. They stared in disbelief. That night I went home and read my *St John's Gospel.* I had taken my first steps to freedom.

"The next morning the reality of the night before slowly dawned on me but my problems and battles with the powers of darkness were far from over. I was being driven mad by voices in my head and Lucifer's audible voice said over and over again I would never be free. I returned again to the crusade meetings I was so desperate to be free and serve Jesus fully. That very night Lucifer stood by my bed. There was no mistaking him. I'd seen him often enough in the past, it was very real indeed. He told me that I belonged to him and to keep away from Christians or I would die. His form and face were black and twisted, his voice ugly with hate and threats. I felt great hairy hands reach out and grab my throat. I tried to shout out, I tried to pray but it was no use. The power of evil was too strong for me. It was all very awful and very real. Then the words of the solo rang in my ears,

> *Only Jesus can take the sin and darkness from me,*
> *Oh! How much He cares for me!*

"As I called upon Jesus Lucifer released his grip on my throat and fled and I decided I would fight with God's help until I was completely free.

"I wandered into many different churches and sometimes heard the blood of Jesus mentioned. At that, a dark force took over me, and strange things occurred. I snatched Bibles and tore them. I knocked communion trays out of the hands of those who were taking around the bread and wine. I would fall to the floor screaming, hissing and slithering like a snake. Then, quite suddenly I would come to myself and remember nothing. Very often I would run out of the church sobbing and crying. After one such incident I ran from the church in total despair and I heard Lucifer's voice say, 'Best to end it all. Die, die, die!' I ran like a tormented, hunted animal down the road. I reached a small bridge and jumped the parapet and was about to throw myself into the water below when a man suddenly pulled me down. I tore myself away and ran again. Blindly I ran into a telephone box, shaking and sobbing for some time. As I grew quieter, I saw on the wall of the telephone box the name and telephone number of a minister, Rev Stanley Jebb.

"Before I even thought, I was on the phone talking to him and being told to come to the church. I met him and two others there and as they prayed for me the powers of darkness again told hold. They were not a bit worried and told me they knew a man, a minister at Burnham-on-Sea, who would help me. His name was Arthur Neil. A meeting was arranged and at last I was on the right road to freedom.

"When I met Arthur Neil I knew instinctively he was a pure and holy man of God. I sat terrified in the chair as the powers within me began to take hold, but somehow I knew all would be well. And after prayer I knew without a shadow of a doubt that the great kingdom of darkness within me was well and truly shaken. However, that night the demons within tormented me telling me to have nothing more to do with Arthur Neil.

"Another meeting was arranged for prayer and ministry and this time many demons left me as they were commanded to go in Jesus' name. I felt happy and free and that night I slept like a baby – the best night's sleep I'd had for many years. A real work was being done but there was still much deliverance to take place as the remaining demons vented their fury as they knew they were in danger of losing the dwelling place they'd occupied for many years.

“Casting out the rest of the demons was a long, exhausting ministry and had to be done at intervals, in special sessions. This was a difficult and tormenting time as I experienced horrific dreams. During the course of my exorcism Mr Neil mentioned Calvary, where Satan and all demons were conquered by Christ. The demons screamed, ‘Don’t speak to me about Calvary. I was there, I was there. I saw it all.’ In spite of all the protests the demons had to go. ‘Jesus is victor!’ said Mr Neil over and over again. After each session, when the demons were gone, I prayed and thanked Jesus for all He had done. I thanked Him with all my heart for setting me free.

She Saw Jesus

“It was at one such session that I actually saw the Lord Jesus Himself, physically standing just behind Mr Neil. The Lord was lovely, arrayed in shining garments and bathed in radiant light, which filled the whole room. His face was gentle and kind. His eyes were filled with deep love, and He was looking straight at me. I knew He loved me. I knew I was His child. He was setting me free. I will never forget it as long as I live. To think that Jesus should appear to someone like me! Ah, the wonder of it all. I needed that vision of Jesus, for the battle had not yet ended. But I knew that as long as I was willing Jesus would complete the great work He had begun.

“This was indeed the case and after several more sessions I was completely free but still needed healing from all the pain and memories I had been through. It was during a time of rest and such healing with a lovely couple, Mr and Mrs Parker in the village of Gamlingay in Bedfordshire, that I saw Jesus again.

"I actually saw Him! This time His hands were outstretched toward me, His eyes were full of love, and He took me in His arms and whispered, 'You are mine.' I knew without a shadow of a doubt that I was His. He would never let me go. He would bring me through all trials, all gloom, until one day I would see Him face to face for all eternity.

"Some weeks later while I was resting and healing I felt the very presence of Jesus in an even greater way than ever before. I felt His presence at first drawing nearer and nearer to my side. Then I heard the audible voice of my Saviour as He whispered sweetly in my ear, 'You are a chaste virgin in my sight. You are my modern Mary Magdalene.' Mr Parker happened to be nearby and saw the expression on my face. He too knew that Jesus was very, very near. He said later that he'd never seen anything like it in his life. My countenance was radiant, he said. Little wonder when Jesus was so near. 'Who is Mary Magdalene?' I asked. With tears in his eyes he read from his Bible how Jesus had cast seven evil spirits from Mary Magdalene, a woman of the city, a street girl, a harlot until Jesus came into her life and changed her completely. Like her I would love Him and serve Him forever."

Doreen was true to her word as she embarked on a ministry of sharing the love and power of Jesus and warning of the dangers of the occult. It is so sad and dangerous that today many who dabble in such things have been exposed to its lure through popular children's books and TV programmes and films. There may well be a terrible harvest that will be reaped in time to come.

I have always found that one of the most moving accounts of Jesus' resurrection is the encounter with Mary Magdalene.

She was a woman of the street whose life was filled with harlotry and demonic forces but Jesus set her free. For those like her and Doreen who may think that they have sunk so low that God could never restore and powerfully use them – think again. Mary was the first person Jesus appeared to after He rose from the dead and she was there when the Holy Spirit came on the Day of Pentecost.

While Doreen Irving's testimony is amazing it is not unique as so many others like her have been wonderfully set free from the powers of darkness in witchcraft and satanism. I have a good friend who had been a witch for more than 20 years powerfully set free in the name of Jesus. Like Doreen before her deliverance, she would come to church but run out whenever songs were sung about the blood of Jesus. An evil power would come over her and she had to get out of the building. She said that after Jesus had set her free the songs she loved to sing most were about the power of the blood of Jesus.

Jesus Christ is the victor over all the powers and forces of darkness. On the cross He crushed the serpent's head. Spiritual warfare therefore is not about trying to gain victory over the devil but to enforce the victory in Christ that has already been won. Doreen mentioned that the demons screamed not to speak about the cross for they said they were there and saw it all. I too have heard demons say this and like with Doreen heard them scream terrified has they left. You can prove the power of what Jesus did at the Calvary, the next time the devil attacks you, submit to God, resist the devil and in Jesus' name all the powers of darkness will flee from you, James 4:7.

I don't know what kind of sinner you may be but I do know what kind of Saviour Jesus is. I don't know what you have done with your life but I know that Jesus gave His for you as He did for Doreen because the greatest need all of us have is for forgiveness.

3

CHRIS LAMBRIANOU

Escape From The Kray Madness

As a young East End tear away, Chris Lambrianou was caught up in the dark world of violent crime, armed robbery, safe blowing, protection rackets, fraud and attempted murder. He became a henchman for the evil Kray twins who terrorized the East End of London during the 1960s.

In the foreword to his book *Escape From the Kray Madness*, Lambrianou's probation officer describes him as a bear of a man, of powerful physique and compelling personality. He says, "It is easy to see the figure he cut in the criminal culture of the sixties which were the years of the London gang wars and ascendency of the notorious Kray twins. By then he had already served several prison sentences, borstal, detention centre and three years at an approved school from the age of eleven."

Lambrianou was convicted at the Old Bailey in 1969 along with the Krays and other members of "The Firm;" he was sentenced to life imprisonment for his part in the murder of Jack the Hat McVitie and was told he would serve a minimum of 15 years.

The following years were a nightmarish existence in maximum security prisons. At times he became like a wild man and was moved from one jail to another in an effort to control him.

By 1975 he had served six years of his sentence and had done a lot of soul searching and read a lot of what he says was enlightening and religious literature. One Sunday evening he was lying on his prison bed listening to the radio and heard the distinctive voice of Bob Dylan singing on a record on a landing below. Chris says, "I tried listening to what was on the radio but the words of the record kept invading my mind, making it hard to concentrate,

'Knock knock knocking on heaven's door...

Ma, take these guns off me...

I can't use them any more...

It's getting dark... Too dark to see...

And I feel I am knocking on heaven's door...'"

He switched off the radio and lay on his bed, eyes closed, thinking how much the words meant to him. 'Take these guns I can't use them anymore,'

Over and over the record played as he lay there thinking of all the wasted years of his life. He says,

"Suddenly, I felt my heart pounding and then it was as if a thick, black cloud descended on my cell enveloping me, an evil clammy darkness so real, so physical, I could almost touch it. I felt blood surging through my veins, a boiling molten scarlet blood and I turned and twisted on my bed fighting the anger, the frightening evil fury, raging inside me. And then the voices started again in my head, 'You are never getting out... You gave your life away to the Krays. You are never getting out. This is forever... Think how you feel now. This emptiness, this nothingness, this loneliness. This is how you are going to feel forever. It's never going to change.'"

Frightened by the voices and the force inside him he jumped off the bed and went to the mirror. He says, "Looking back at me was a scowling, snarling, sneering beast, shocking in its ugliness and it was screaming, 'Kill yourself, you're never getting out. End it all.'"

Somewhere else in what he called his twisted soul he heard another voice, faint but insistent, pleading with him to drag himself out of the madness, to do something positive to break the evil spell before it pulled him over the line and past the point of no return.

He then remembered some books given to him by another prisoner and went to a box under his bed where his eyes fell on a Gideon Bible which he didn't know was there. He says,

"I threw it down and looked for something else. I went through a dozen books and then for some reason I could not understand, I found myself picking up the Bible again. I started reading in Genesis but gave up after a couple of minutes however I couldn't let the book go. I didn't know what it was but there was something there, a power. I put the Bible under my pillow, thinking that if there were any good thoughts in the book, they would come through to me. I lay in the darkness, exhausted but unable to sleep. I kept thinking of the Bible, saying over and over to myself, 'If there is anybody there, let me know. I don't believe, but if there is someone there, please let me know.' I didn't feel comfortable with the

Bible under the pillow. I wanted it nearer. I took it and clutched it against my heart and closed my eyes, fighting to control the rage burning inside me. Finally, mercifully, I dropped off to sleep. It was around three in the morning, I had been fighting the devil for nine hours."

When he awoke he took the Bible with him stuffed down his trousers. He had an overwhelming desire to have it close to him all day. He started reading it secretly in his cell and thinking about Jesus more and more. At the end of each day he would get down on his hands and knees and pray thanking the Lord for the day. He says, "I was not a religious fanatic and I was not off my trolley. I felt I was the sanest I'd been in my whole life."

A few months later he was moved to a new prison. He was still reading the Bible but the 'raging beast' was still in him if things did not go his way.

One night, as he lay on his bed, he began to cry thick tears of remorse for the world he had lost and destroyed and for all the loved ones he had left in pain. He describes what happened next,

"And then, through my tears, I saw three people in the corner of the cell. They looked Middle Eastern and wearing dark raincoats. The one in the middle, the only one I clearly remember, had long, jet black hair and a trimmed beard; under his raincoat, he was wearing a European suit with a white shirt and tie. And he had the most wonderful, warm welcoming eyes I'd ever seen. He had such a clarity of vision I knew he was a man of purpose. Through my tears, I said to him, 'How do I put it right? I have run through my life, wrecking everything. I've made a terrible, terrible mess. I'm so sorry.' The bearded man (who he said later he knew was Jesus) said simply, 'follow

us' then he and the other two men vanished as quickly as they had come."

He started attending church in the prison as his life began to turn around. His life and attitude so changed overtime that he was granted parole. His faith and witness became stronger and he managed to get work at the Ley Community in Oxfordshire, a rehabilitation centre for alcohol and drug abusers.

At the end of his fascinating book he says, "I'm proud of what I am achieving at the Ley. I'm proud that I had the courage to write this book. And I'm proud to be a Christian. With God's guidance, I shall continue to be one. The prodigal son said, *'Shall I leave the swine and return to my father's house, perhaps he will give me a job on the land. When he was far off his father saw him and ran to greet him,'"* Luke 15:11-32.

4

SADHU SUNDAR SINGH

India's Holy Man

The name of Sundar Singh may not be known to many but in India, his homeland, and the East he is a spiritual legend and as well known as Billy Graham is in the West. His life and ministry have had an enormous impact and his legacy of being totally surrendered to Jesus Christ has been and still is an inspiration to millions.

Raised a devout Sikh, and consecrated from his youth to become a Hindu *Sadhu* (a Hindu who devotes his entire life to his religion and forsakes all worldly pleasures) his spiritual longings were not fulfilled until emotional and spiritual turmoil drove him to urgently ask the true living God to reveal Himself, lest he take his own life in the hope of finding peace in the next. He had an awesome encounter with Jesus Christ and thereafter lived an amazing life with Him and for Him.

Family and Religious Background

On September 3, 1889, Sundar Singh was born to Sher Singh of Rampur, Punjab, in northern India. His mother, a deeply religious woman, nurtured him in the traditions of the Sikhs. Sundar often spoke of his mother with much love and respect because of the good foundation she laid for his life. He was raised in the luxury of his family's wealth. As a Sikh Sundar was taught about Hinduism and went along with his parents to Hindu and Sikh temples. By the age of seven he had already memorized the *Bhagavadgita*, the intricate Hindu dialogue containing spiritual life lessons. At sixteen, not only had he mastered the *Vedas*, the ancient sacred books of Hinduism, but he had also read the Koran, the sacred book of Islam. He then became acquainted with some *Sadhus* who taught him *Yoga*.

After his dramatic conversion, during which he encountered the risen Jesus, Sundar travelled all over India wearing a yellow robe without having any permanent residence. His life was remarkable in its Christ-likeness.

In 1906, he went to Tibet for the first time. The country attracted him, primarily because of the great opposition there to evangelism. He knew it was dangerous and told those who warned him against the dangers and the fierce persecution he would face and that he might never leave there alive, “I never expect to return from Tibet.” But return from there he did year after year but not without suffering terrible attacks and incredible deliverances.

In 1914, he was preaching in Nepal, a country with very strong roots in Buddhism. In the town of Rasa, he was sentenced to death by a local Lama on the grounds of spreading a foreign religion. Sundar knew his trial would have but one end because cruelty was the mark of the people, their forms of execution well illustrating the spirit of their religion.

The victim may either be sown inside a wet yak-skin which was left in the heat of the sun to dry and shrink until the person within was crushed slowly and agonizingly to death, or he may be thrown into a deep, dry well, on top of the corpses which have been cast there before him, to die of starvation and disease.

Sundar found himself dragged to the well because he had been preaching the Gospel, the top was lifted and the violent, angry people crowded round him, beating and thrashing him until at last a violent blow sent him headlong into the pit the top of which was then covered and locked. He was without food and drink, naked inside the well together with the corpses of executed murderers. He was there for three days and nights when suddenly he heard a sound at the top of the well with a key turning in the lock and the lid opening. A moment later a rope touched his face which he grasped and so made his way to freedom. Once out he fell to the ground exhausted and when he looked around his deliverer had gone. He found a safe place to sleep the night and at dawn he bathed to rid himself of the terrible smell of death and returned to the market place to preach. He was again arrested and taken before the Grand Lama who questioned him over and over again as to who had helped him escape and how they got the key and where was it now? There was only one key to the well which should be around the Lama's waist on his key ring. When he checked his face fell and he was furious and ordered the waiting monks to take Sundar away and set him free. The key of the well was still on his own ring.

Sundar Singh journeyed not only to Tibet but all over India and Ceylon (modern day Sri Lanka) . Between 1918-1919, he visited Malaysia, Japan and China. Between 1920-1922 he went to Western Europe, Australia and Israel. He preached in many cities – Jerusalem, Lima, Berlin and Amsterdam among others. His last journey took him back to Tibet. He was still just forty but his health was failing and he had lost much of the strength he once knew. In April 1929 he made his way through the 18,000 foot passes that lead from India into Tibetan territory. It was a journey full of danger with immense rocks on one side and precipices on the other with sheer drops for thousands of feet. Wearing his dark glasses as protection from the glare of the snow and carrying a staff he journeyed this time never to return. Like his master he willingly gave his all to reach out with God's love.

His Encounter with Christ December 3, 1903

After Sundar's beloved mother died when he was just fourteen-years-old, his life changed dramatically. He grew increasingly despairing and aggressive. Convinced that what Jesus had taught was completely wrong, he hated the Bible, threw stones at preachers and encouraged others to do likewise. His hatred of the local missionaries and Christians culminated in the public burning of a Bible which he tore apart page by page and threw into the flames.

Three days after this he woke up at three o'clock in the morning and went out into the moonlit courtyard for the ceremonial bath observed by devout Hindus and Sikhs before worship. But however hard he tried, he couldn't find the peace he had been searching for in his own religion. He had reached a point in his life where committing suicide crossed his mind and he decided to kill himself if God did not reveal to him the true way of peace.

He returned to his room and knelt down, bowed his head to the ground and pleaded that God would reveal Himself. Yet nothing happened so he planned

to throw himself in front of a train, the Ludhiana express that passed by at 5am every morning behind his house, in the hope that he would find peace in his future reincarnation as a good Hindu.

There were still a couple of hours before the train was due and he cried, "Oh God, if there be a God, reveal Thyself before I die." Time passed. Then he was rather surprised to see a faint cloud of light in the room. It was too early for the dawn. He opened the door and peered out to the courtyard. Darkness. Turning back into the room he saw that the light in the room was getting brighter. At first he feared that the room was on fire. He then thought that it might be an answer to his prayer. To his sheer amazement he saw not the face of any of his traditional gods, but of Jesus the Christ who was there in the room, shining, radiating an inexpressible joy and peace and love.

This is how Sundar described what happened next,

> **"Jesus spoke to me, He said, 'How long will you persecute me? I died for you. I have come to save you. You were praying to know the right way; why do you not take it? I am the Way.' 'He spoke in Hindustani, and He spoke to me.'**
>
> **"I fell at His feet. How long I knelt I cannot say. But as I rose the vision faded. It was no thought of mine that called Him there. I had bathed. I was not thinking of Him or desiring Him. Had it been Krishna, or one**

of my own gods, I might have expected it – but not Jesus.

"I ran to tell my father what had happened and said, 'I am a Christian. I can serve no one else but Jesus.'"

This is what he later said about knowing Jesus,

* "There is a great difference between knowing about Jesus and knowing Him...There is no difference between nominal Christians and non-Christians. When we know Him everything is different and we are living in a new world – a new atmosphere. Heaven begins on earth for us. Those who know Him know that Jesus is everything to them. They can bear witness because they have been living with Him."

* "When I used to know about Jesus Christ I used to hate Him because I didn't understand Him; but since I know Him I bear witness and I am not ashamed to suffer. I wish I could show you my heart – I have such peace in my heart."

* "Christ is not merely a great man who is dead and gone; He is the incarnation of God, the Saviour of the world. We must live in Him – then we shall have a message for the world and we shall see Him again in glory. We shall be crowned in this world. It is such a joy to live for Him and bring others to Him."

* "I was going to commit suicide. Hinduism (offered) no spiritual help. Prayer is the most essential thing. Without prayer we cannot understand Jesus. Many know about Him but they do not live in Him."

5

MOUSSA KONÉ

Finding Jesus Through The Koran

Moussa is from the Ivory Coast in West Africa and was desperately searching for the assurance of salvation. Like many Muslims he was afraid of going to hell, but was tortured by a promiscuous lifestyle and could not find freedom from the heavy chains that bound him.

Deliverance did come as Moussa received the Lord Jesus Christ as his personal Saviour through studying the Koran and by a visitation from a "supernatural being."

He says, "I was looking for my salvation like a sick person seeks healing, but I could not find an effective remedy in the Koran even though I studied through all of the 114 suras (chapters). I examined them one by one, and there was not one that could tell me with undeniable certainty that I would go to paradise."

He searched the Koran for answers and assurance and made an amazing discovery.

"I opened my Koran to sura 2, where it says, *'Say ye: We believe in God, and the revelation given to us, and to Abraham, Ishmael, Isaac, Jacob and the Tribes, and that given to Moses and Jesus, that given to (all) Prophets from their Lord; We made no difference between one and another of them and to Him do we submit.'*

"Now I understood that God gave His book to Moses and Jesus. The Koran was therefore telling me not to make any distinction between these books and that of Muslims and to submit myself to the will of God."

Moussa continued his meditations in the Koran and read in the fifth sura vs 46:

"And in their footsteps we sent Jesus the son of Mary, confirming the Law that had come before him. We sent him the Gospel: Therein was guidance and light and confirmation of the Law that had come before him: a guidance and an admonition to those who fear God."

Moussa was deeply touched by the fact that the Koran declared God Himself gave the Gospel to Jesus, and that the Gospel is the guidance and the light for all the people.

Moussa decided to continue his research on the person of Jesus, "Koran commentators agree that 'holy' means 'without sin.' In the 114 suras, I discovered that five titles are attributed to Jesus. These titles are different from those applied to others and are, in fact, greater than the titles of all the others. He is called (1) the Messiah, and (2) the Son of Mary, because nobody knew Him to have a human father. Mohammed is called the 'son of Abdullah,' but Jesus is called (3) the Apostle of God, (4) the Spirit of God and (5) the Word of God, one of those close to God, who was honoured on this earth and beyond.

"In the 114 suras of the Koran, no sin is attributed to Jesus. Adam's sin can be found in verse 36 (in some translations) of the second sura; the sin of Moses in sura 28, and Jonah's sin is mentioned in sura 37. In sura 40, [verse 55 according to some translations] Mohammed is commanded *'to ask protection and forgiveness for your fault.'*

"I said to myself, 'Even my beloved Mohammed sinned! So how is it that Jesus never sinned? Why is He above all the other prophets?'"

At first Moussa was indignant and jealous for his faith, but he could not help but respect Jesus. He marvelled that Jesus had actually lived on this earth for 33 years, and yet there is no record of any of His sins! During this time some Christians approached Moussa. They claimed that Jesus was crucified and that their sins had been forgiven as a result of His sacrifice.

"The Koran asserts in the third sura verse 48 (or 55 according to some translations), *'God said to Jesus: I will make you taste death, I will raise you unto me.'* When I pondered that statement, 'I will make you taste death,' I said to myself, 'This resembles the crucifixion!' And the words, 'I will raise you unto me' reminded me of the resurrection from the dead and Jesus' ascension to heaven to sit at the right hand of God!"

Appearance of a Supernatural Being

"After all these revelations, I did not know what to do. I tried to go out in the evenings but it was no longer exciting. I could not eat. I was morose because I knew I was not saved. Therefore, one evening I said, 'If these trials I am going through are of God, then He should prove it to me physically. He should show me what to do.' That evening I spoke to God in Jula, my native language and not in Arabic this time. I told him this, 'My father is an Imam (mosque leader). When I am with him, I lead the prayers. All my uncles are Imams. I am the descendant of an Imam. For that reason, I cannot abandon Islam.'

"I then turned off the light but all of a sudden another light appeared in my room. Someone was there. Initially I was scared but afterwards his presence did not frighten me any longer. The Being in question approached me and placed his hand on my right shoulder. I remember that episode as though it happened only yesterday.

"He spoke to me, saying that all I needed to know had already been revealed to me and it was my personal decision to either believe or not. After this, everything became dark again. I looked all over the room for this Being but I could not find him anywhere.

"Eventually I knocked on the door of my neighbour, a Dane. He came out of his room, his eyes reddened by sleep. He appeared drunk. I asked him if he had been to my room a few seconds earlier. He answered, 'Are you crazy? What could I have come to your room for at such a time?' I apologized. I could not sleep the whole night as I was overwhelmed by the vision.

The Koran Burns

"The following evening, after eating and praying, I made the same request to God. I took the Koran and recited the Yassin sura. I did not know I was challenging God thus, and that when you challenge God, he shows you who he really is. I was reading when I suddenly saw a live coal in the right page of my Koran. Before I could react, another live coal had appeared. Two live coals were burning up my Koran. Afterwards there were several others. I was sitting on my bed with my legs crossed and with my back to the wall. The Koran began to burn. I looked up and there was indeed a ceiling between the room and the sky. So where were these live coals coming from?

"I was afraid, but not for my security. I was afraid because the holy book of Islam, the book of every Muslim, the book that I was holding, was burning. This book which is the compass of a billion people in the world, a book in which about fifty percent of the population of the Ivory Coast have put their faith, was going up in flames!

"By the time I expected to feel the burning in my hands, everything had burned up, despite the Koran's hardback cover. There were only ashes left in my hand. That day I felt he greatest terror in my life. I have never been so afraid. This episode took thirty minutes. I remained seated at the same spot and did not sleep until morning.

"I spent four sleepless nights because I was resisting sleep, but on the fifth day, I could no longer resist. I was overcome by a deep sleep. I woke up late the next day.

"During that sleep, I had a dream in which, I saw a tall man standing opposite me. He had bright eyes like car headlights and I was dazzled by this light. He was approaching me. I was afraid, very much afraid, but suddenly my fear gave way to courage and I went to meet him. As I was about to touch him, he stopped and I asked for his name. He refused to tell me who he was. He rather began reciting the Islamic creed: 'Laila la la ho: Mohammed rassoula lah.' Then he retreated and disappeared. I woke up with a start and realized at that precise moment that there was something in me that was stronger than what was in him.

"In the morning, at work, I was more relaxed. I had the impression that there was a change in my life. I had more strength and my nights became normal.

"Drawing the conclusion from all I had gone through, I found that there is no salvation in the Koran and that the Pentateuch and the Gospel are books from God. I also realized that Jesus is a Prophet above all prophets, that He is sinless, and that He was crucified.

"I had asked God to give me some physical proof. There was this physical vision, the burning of the Koran and next, this Being, symbolizing Islam, which fled in my dream."

Moussa decided to make a commitment to Jesus Christ. His prayer was so sincere that for the first time he knew that he had really talked with God. He confessed his sins. Suddenly, he closed his eyes and says as in a film, "I saw passing before my eyes all the sins I had ever committed in night clubs, my indecent sins, the sins of invoking spirits for money and so on. This vision lasted at least ten minutes, during which time many of my sins passed before my eyes. But I also knew that Jesus Christ had entered my life and that it was He who had given me forgiveness of all those sins and an indescribable joy."

Moussa's Plea to his Muslim Brother

"I hope I have helped you to discover the source of this indescribable joy through this brief testimony. You saw my determination to follow the Koran in spite of the contradictions I detected in it. You saw to what extent I was attached to the religion of my fathers. However, I thank God for giving me the strength to say yes to the truth proclaimed by the Bible.

"Muslim friend, what are you going to do?

"Will you follow the "uncertainties" of the Koran or will you go to the side of the one who is the truth, Jesus Christ, who assures you of salvation now and, of course, in the hereafter?

"When you have been deceived in all areas and in different ways, just do not accept that, for the sake of the salvation of your soul. Do not trust in the mere words of an Imam but take the Koran and scrutinize it, study it. Whether you are called Abdoulaye, Moussa, Maimouna, Fatou, Bakary or any other name, do not say, 'Because my father is Muslim, I am also Muslim.' Ask yourself whether you are saved. If you die today, will you go to Paradise? That is the question you have to answer.

"You will certainly discover in your Koran research that you might be able to be saved through your good deeds, but think a while: Are you sure you can do enough good deeds to gain a place in Paradise? As you do good deeds, you also do evil ones which God sees. That is why the Koran cannot assure you of salvation. You will only find "uncertainties" in the Koran whereas the Bible which, besides, is confirmed by the Koran, shows you the path above all others, the only path.

"Do not look at your fortune or your social rank. Do not look at those around you. Look at your own life. The important thing is for your sins to be forgiven, and the only way for that to happen is through Jesus. He forgives your sins, even those you have committed since your youth. Does the Koran not say that those who follow Jesus are above those who do not believe in him?

"My Muslim friend, what are you going to do?

"'Come! Follow me!' Jesus said.

"Will you do it?"

6

FRED WERTHEIM

Jesus My Messiah

Fred was born in Germany in 1925, the son of a baker, he lived in a small village of about 2,000 people. By the time he was eight, the Aryan philosophy of Hitler was well on its way to acceptance by most Germans. Fred's best friends did not want to play with him anymore because he was Jewish. His parents, who were prospering in the bakery business, held to the illusion that Hitler would lose his popularity and that things would get better once again for the Jews. Instead they got worse.

On July 2, 1938, Fred became *bar mitzvah*. He was the last Jewish boy to undergo the ceremony in his district. Four months later came *Kristallnacht* (night of broken glass), his synagogue, along with hundreds of others, was destroyed. Six days later, it was ordered that Jewish children were to be expelled from the schools. At the same time, Jewish males that were thirteen or older were being conscripted for "labour camps." Fred was small for his age and because of his size was overlooked. Before long, entire Jewish families were being deported to the death camps. Yet, for some mysterious reason, his family was spared. Their immigration number came up, enabling them to leave Germany and in May of 1941 the Wertheim's left what had become Hitler's Germany. They travelled by way of France, Spain and Portugal and arrived on the shores of America.

Fred learned the English language quickly and after being in the States only two years, he was drafted into the US Army. The eighteen-year-old went through basic training and was shipped out to England taking part in the invasion of Europe on D-Day. He fought his way through France and across the Rhine River, ironically, into his native Germany. Then Fred and some of his fellow Army soldiers were captured and taken to a prisoner of war camp near Hanover–Stalag 11B. Many of the prisoners had been there throughout most of the war and were very weak. Some couldn't even stand up. No work was assigned to the prisoners, for it would have probably killed most of them. Each morning, Fred and the others answered a roll call and then spent the rest of the day wandering within the boundaries of the high wire fences. The conditions in the camp were horrendous.

Meanwhile, back in the States, Fred's family received a telegram, it was from the War Department saying that Fred was missing in action. Germany didn't turn over names of prisoners, so his family had no way of knowing if he was alive.

Eventually the Allied Forces conquered Germany and General Montgomery's Ninth Division liberated Stalag 11B. Fred first had to recuperate from tapeworm and other maladies received as a result of his imprisonment. Then, around Mother's Day of 1945, he was sent home to a great reception.

Fred felt very grateful to be back in a safe place. He couldn't forget, however, the horrors of war or the miracle of his preservation. "God has done so many good things for me. He brought my immediate family out of Germany. He kept me alive in a prisoner of war camp. And there was the time that I was in a German halftrack that turned over on top of me. Two Germans lay dead next to me. The halftrack was so heavy with equipment that I couldn't move. Then water started to come up as we were pressed down in a field. I thought my life was over. I said the *Sh'ma* and I spoke to God pleading for His help. At that moment, several of my German captors were able to lift the halftrack and slide me out from under it. I was safe once again."

Fred Wertheim believed God had preserved him for a purpose. He married a Jewish girl from his synagogue and he and Laura settled down in the Bronx. They raised two sons and things were going fine until he got a phone call from his oldest son Steve who had moved to California after graduating from college. Fred could not believe his ears, but Steve's words were clear, "Dad, Mom, I've come to believe in Jesus as the Messiah."

Fred took the news very hard. "After all I had been through, here I saw my own flesh and blood had turned against me," he said. Fred worked as a mail carrier, and for weeks after the phone call he would just suddenly start crying on his route. People asked him what was wrong, but he couldn't tell them. He was ashamed to let them know that his son had become a Christian.

Steve tried to explain to his father that his decision to believe in Jesus was not intended to hurt him. He told him about a Mr Goldstein who had originally spoke to him about Jesus. Goldstein was a "Jew for Jesus" who Steve had met through Bible study meetings.

When his son said that Mr Goldstein was coming to New York and wanted to visit him, Fred agreed. He said to his son, "I want to meet the man who did this to you and I want to kill him." Goldstein and his wife visited the Wertheims and instead of a violent or angry exchange, the two couples discussed things over coffee.

Mrs Wertheim says, “We asked them many questions. After a while, Mr Goldstein pointed out prophecies in the Jewish Bible. I was a little shocked to see that my husband was very curious to know more.”

Fred Wertheim's curiosity continued past that evening. He started attending Bible study meetings in New York,

“I became a very conscientious student. Each week we were asked to prepare for the next lesson by reading a particular passage from the Scriptures. One week the assignment was to read the first letter of John (in the New Testament), but I read the Gospel of John by mistake. I couldn't put it down. Then, on the morning of September 29, 1975, I woke up at four o'clock. I saw what was the outline of a figure standing in the doorway of my bedroom. I couldn't see a face, but I knew it was Jesus. I was convinced that He was real and that I wanted Him in my life. I knew He was my Messiah. For me to become a believer, it took a supernatural event like this one. I know it's not that way for everybody who believes in Jesus, but that's how it happened to me. I didn't tell my wife until later in the day.”

Fred’s wife was upset about the news. First her son and now her husband! To compound things their youngest son, Robbie, announced that he too was a believer. He didn't want to say anything until his father came to believe because he was afraid that it would be too traumatic an experience for Fred. In Robbie's words, “I didn't think he could take another one.”

But could Laura Wertheim take another family member believing in Jesus? She says, “I was very stubborn. While I felt surrounded by believers, I kept reminding myself that so many people were killed in the Holocaust. So many Jews were killed. I couldn't betray my upbringing.”

Then the Wertheim family went to see a movie called *The Hiding Place*. Laura watched the true story about a Christian woman and her family in Holland who during the war helped save the lives of Jews. Says Laura, "It showed the suffering this woman went through, yet she kept her faith in God. It made me see that God was working during the Holocaust – through people like this dear woman. Because she believed in Jesus she helped the Jews. I just sat there and wept and sobbed through the entire picture."

The next week she too accepted Jesus as her Messiah.

Fred later summed up his life like this, "First I escaped from Hitler as a Jewish refugee. Then I was liberated as an American prisoner of war. But I was never free until Jesus my Messiah saved and rescued me."

The Damascus Road

Another Jew who came to know Jesus as his Messiah through a supernatural encounter was the Apostle Paul. He was journeying from Jerusalem to Damascus with letters from the High Priest to persecute and imprison Christians he found there. His life was radically transformed when he saw Jesus on that Damascus road. Paul was struck blind by the encounter and had to be led into the city by his hand.

> *"As he neared Damascus on his journey, suddenly a light from heaven flashed around him. He fell to the ground and heard a voice say to him, 'Saul, Saul, why do you persecute me?' 'Who are you, Lord?'* Saul asked. *'I am Jesus, whom you are persecuting,'* he replied. *'Now get up and go into the city, and you will be told what you must do,'"* Acts 9:3-6.

The Lord also spoke directly to another man at this time. He was a follower of Jesus and named Ananias. He was told to go and pray for Paul to receive his sight but objected knowing Paul's reputation. But the Lord said to him,

> *"Go! This man is my chosen instrument to carry my name before the Gentiles and their kings and before the people of Israel. I will show him how much he must suffer for my name,"* Acts 9:15,16.

When Ananias came to pray for Paul he used two of the most beautiful words in the entire Bible, *"Brother Saul."* Since God had accepted Saul, so he became Ananias's brother in Christ.

Paul's encounter with Jesus transformed his theological understanding of what took place at the cross. The law of God stated, *"Anyone who is hung on a tree is under God's curse,"* Deuteronomy 21:23. Man could only take the punishment so far and then it was seen to be carried further by God. Ciaphas the High priest and others knew this and so they decided the best way to kill the memory of Jesus and all He had done was for the people to see Him being made a curse by God. There would be no legends and no martyrs. No one would believe His claims to be the Son of God or believe He was the promised Messiah despite all the miracles and signs and wonders if He was seen as cursed.

Yet all this was part of the plan of God. Sin brought with it a curse and only by Jesus becoming a curse could its penalty be paid. This is what the Apostle Paul came to understand and changed him from being a persecutor of the church to becoming a preacher of the cross. He wrote,

> *"Christ redeemed us from the curse of the law by becoming a curse for us, for it is written: 'Cursed is everyone who is hung on a tree,'"*
>
> Galatians 3:13

He also knew that because Jesus was who He claimed to be God had vindicated Him and raised Him to life. Jesus was alive and Paul had seen Him, this is why Paul came to glory in the cross and wrote later to the church at Rome,

> *"Regarding his Son, who as to his human nature was a descendant of David, and who through the Spirit of holiness was declared with power to be the Son of God by his resurrection from the dead: Jesus Christ our Lord,"* Romans 1:3-4.

Paul also gives us an intriguing insight into his conversion at the end of the book of Romans where he lists his friends and thanks them.

> *"Greet Andronicus and Junias, my relatives who have been in prison with me. They are outstanding among the apostles, and they were in Christ before I was,"* Romans 16:7.

What would you do if you had come to know Jesus as your Messiah and had a relative like Paul who was so misguided but zealous for his faith?

"Lord, open his eyes and let him know who Jesus really is!"

7

A PASSION FOR JESUS

Ram Bali Singh has ministered at the church I pastor on two occasions and each time we were conscious of listening to a man who walked with God. He came highly commended by a good friend who had spent time with him in India and seen first hand the amazing work God is doing through him planting churches in villages all over the country.

Ram is only small in physical stature, about four foot ten inches tall and slim build, but he is a giant in the spirit. He shares amusingly how he thanks God for the way He made him small of stature, as on one occasion a Hindu extremist was hired to kill him. He fired a shot at Ram and it missed him hitting a wall behind him just four inches straight above his head. He knew who the would be assassin was and was going to report him to the police but as the man begged for mercy, Ram said he would not report him on the condition he attended his Bible study every Friday night. The would be killer was there each week and after about a month he gave his life to Jesus Christ. A few weeks later his wife and children and whole family came to know Jesus as Saviour and Ram tells of his joy in baptising them all. Smith Wigglesworth used to say that he was a hundred times bigger on the inside than on the outside and the same can be said for Ram Bali Singh.

When he was 21 -years-old Ram describes how he was on a spiritual journey to find the truth. He had been an atheist for many years but had in recent years become a devout Hindu. He was witnessed to by some Christians and given a tract to read about Jesus Christ and the Christian faith. At first he was hostile but he came to realise that Christianity had a great deal to offer and began to embrace its teachings.

He tells how soon after one night while in Delhi he had the most amazing encounter with Jesus. It was between midnight and 1am in the morning when a strong, cold wind came in through his bedroom window. He immediately knew this was extremely unusual because it was so hot that time of year. When he looked up he saw a bright light coming towards him in the shape of a human figure. He realised this was God revealing Himself to him and even though he couldn't see the features he knew it was Jesus.

As he stared astonished at the person in the light he heard Him say, "I am Jesus," and three times Jesus repeated, "Abide in me and follow me." Then the light faded and Jesus left the room. It was a life changing encounter and Ram couldn't wait to tell his best friend what had happened. When he did he was in for another shock. His friend told him that on the very same night he had a dream in which Jesus came to him in a blaze of light and said exactly the same things.

That was over 25 years ago and today Ram is still abiding in Jesus and following Him. He is the senior pastor of New Life Church in Ranchi in the North East province of India.

Sheik Mohamid Amin was born in the Juna Province of Ethiopia to the son of a goatherder and a mother who was barren for many years. She was so desperate for children that she promised God that if He gave her a son he would become the servant of the Lord.

From childhood, Mohamid studied the Koran and later won a scholarship to study in Saudi Arabia. While there he began to pray fervently to God looking for direction and the inner peace he so desperately desired.

Nine years later he returned to his native Ethiopia where his dream was to spread Islam in his own land and all over the world. He earned a position in one of the largest mosques but later went to study further in the Sudan returning to Ethiopia when he was 30 but with his health in tatters. He admitted reluctantly that even though he was highly respected as a teacher, privately his life was full of sin. He had slept with many prostitutes and now had AIDS. For four months he was totally bedridden and his family made preparations for his funeral.

Then something amazing and miraculous happened. While in hospital, Mohamid saw a bright light and Jesus appeared to him dressed in a doctor's coat. He said, "Mohamid, rise up!"

Mohamid was initially shocked and then confused, he felt too ill to do anything but then Jesus touched his sick body, took his hand, and sat down next to him on the bed. Mohamid said, "Jesus seemed to know my every thought."

In just a week Mohamid was walking again and he has in his possession a certificate from the hospital stating that there was no longer any sign whatsoever of him being HIV positive. Today he is a full time Christian evangelist ministering in churches all over Ethiopia.

Paul Ciniraj found a piece of a Christian tract in his notebook. It still remains a mystery how it found its way there. He said, "I was about to throw it into a dustbin when my eyes caught the following words, *'For the wages of sin is death, but the gift of God is eternal life in Christ Jesus our Lord'* (Romans 6:23). These words made me feel uneasy. Still in spite of myself I read on, *'Here is a trustworthy saying that deserves full acceptance: Christ Jesus came into the world to save sinners - of whom I am the worst,'* (1 Timothy 1:15). Until this moment I was convinced that I was not a bad man, and led my life in a proper way. But now, all of a sudden, I was full of doubts about my attitudes, intentions and conduct.

"I went to bed, but was restless and could not sleep for a long time. When I finally fell asleep, I had a very strange and disturbing vision: One by one, all the transgressions and violations I had committed since my childhood began to appear before me, like the scenes in a movie. Then each one of them transformed into a blister on my body, till I was completely covered with festering sores. I felt unbearable pain. Realising not what I was doing I cried out, 'God! Hear me! Save me!'

"Then, a person surrounded by bright light came down from heaven and touched me. I understood that He was Jesus, the one whom I had been waging a war against. His touch was pleasant, it cooled both my body and mind. I closed my eyes with a heavenly joy, and when I finally opened them again, I saw that all the blisters and sores had disappeared from my body. But Jesus, who came in bright and spotless, was now infested with my sores. I immediately understood the meaning of this vision, although it was only later, when I began to study the Bible, that I read this verse in the Bible, *'Christ was without sin, but for our sake God made him share in our sin in*

***order that in union with him we might share the righteousness of God,'* (2 Corinthians 5:21). I woke up a new man.**

"At once I shared my experience with my father and mother with great joy. But my mother said it was not from God, but a trick of *Iblis* (Satan). I was fully convinced however, that God the Heavenly Father made me as a new creation and His own child by the power of salvation of His only begotten son Jesus Christ through the Holy Spirit. Later, my family too believed in the Lord Jesus Christ and suffered hardships because of their precious faith in Him."

8

ERNIE HOLLANDS

A Radical Change

ERNIE HOLLANDS
HEBRON
Ministries Inc.
www.hebron.ca
A non-profit organization
dedicated to bringing
FREEDOM TO PRISONERS
through faith in
Jesus Christ
P.O. Box 1505, London
Ontario, Canada
N6A 5M2
519-641-4062

Ernie Hollands was born in 1930 in the slums of Halifax, Nova Scotia, Canada. He had no memory of being loved or embraced as a child as his home was full of pain as alcoholism and poverty took control.

His life of crime began at just eight-years of age when his mother took him shopping and taught him how to steal. By the age of nine he was stealing guns and ammunition and at 12 he was placed in a reform school. The inevitable cycle of crime continued and when he was just 16 he was imprisoned for crimes such as breaking and entering, bank robbery, and attempted murder of a police officer. In total Ernie spent 25 years of combined sentences in prisons across Canada and the

USA. He escaped from prison five times, and was labelled an *"habitual criminal"* and one of the most wanted men in Canada.

It seemed as if there was no hope for a man like Ernie Hollands. But something was about to change. During his prison term in Millhaven Penitentiary in Bath, Ontario, Ernie began to make fish flies and was so good that he developed quite a successful business. In 1975 one of his business contacts, a sports store owner named Grant Bailey, began to reach out to Ernie and urged him to read the Bible and become a Christian. He also offered to buy fish flies from Ernie to sell in his sports store in Pembroke, Ontario. At first Ernie showed little interest in reading the Bible or anything else Christian but Grant's kindness and friendship caused him to reconsider his initial hostility to the idea and so gradually Ernie took an interest in Christian things and started to read the Bible.

Up to now his life had been filled with violence and he was hard both on the inside as well as on the outside but he was about to have an encounter with God that would literally blow his mind as well as transform his life.

It took place on March 12, 1975, at two o'clock in the morning when Ernie awoke with a deep sense of conviction that he should confess his sins to God. As he wept his way to God he felt that his past had been truly forgiven. But something even more dramatic was about to take place. As he got to his feet he turned to look at his cell door but somehow what he now saw was no longer the dark interior of his cell but the room of a house with a door on the right side of it, positioned where the cell door was located. This door opened and Jesus walked through it straight towards Ernie who tells what happened next,

"Jesus stood in front of me. He was wearing white and of medium height. He touched me on the left

shoulder (which I felt) and said three things. (Ernie said these statements sounded as though they came from inside himself, he was not aware of the movement of Jesus' lips as they were uttered, but the voice was like thunder.)

"Jesus first said, 'I'm so glad you didn't kill that police officer,' and then He smiled. (This referred to the time years before when in the course of a supermarket robbery in Hollywood, California, Ernie had struggled with a policeman for control of a stolen gun, and in the brawl he accidentally shot the officer in the leg. Ernie then gave himself up, hoping that the policeman would perhaps shoot him and put him out of his misery. Instead he found himself incarcerated in Los Angeles until he was released to the Canadian authorities for crimes he had committed in Canada.)

"Then Jesus said, 'Your slate is now wiped clean,' and He moved His hands in a way that suggested something was being erased. The third thing Jesus went on to say was, 'Now you can start all over again,' making a semicircular motion with His arms, to suggest that I was beginning a brand new life."

Then Jesus disappeared.

The Scripture, *"Therefore, if anyone is in Christ, he is a new creation; the old has gone, the new has come!"* 2 Corinthians 5:17, became a reality in Ernie's new life.

By an incredible miracle just a year later in 1976 Ernie was released from prison! His first job was working in Bailey's Sports Store, where he helped Mr Bailey and continued to make his fish flies. He soon began working with troubled teens on the streets and eventually he began speaking in schools, meetings, churches, and prisons everywhere, telling people about the love of God that had transformed his life so completely.

Throughout the years Ernie spoke to hundreds of thousands of people in Canada, the US, and many other countries, including the United Kingdom, Bermuda, Spain, New Zealand, Japan, and Africa. Everywhere he went he testified that Jesus Christ had the power to change lives.

Ernie also began writing about his amazing life story. His first book, called *Hooked*, was released in 1982. He then established *Ernie Hollands Hebron Ministries*, which was incorporated in 1983. That same year the Hebron Farm was opened, a place dedicated to helping people receive freedom through a relationship with God. The farm was expanded and relocated to London, Ontario, in 1986. In 1991 Ernie's second book, *Prison Chains Broken,* was released. Since that time it has been translated into French, Braille and Indonesian.

From 1977 to the present the ministry carries on correspondence with prison inmates all over the world, sharing God's love with them.

In 1996 Ernie passed away into the presence of the One who has so transformed his life.

Prison inmates listening to Ernie give his testimony

Bringing Christmas treats to inmates at a prison in Peterborough, Ontario, Canada

9

GULSHAN ESTHER

The Torn Veil

It was in the spring of 1966 that Gulshan made a desperate visit to England to see if there was any medical hope for her recovery. When she was just six-months-old typhoid left her a cripple and now 14 years later her devoted father took her to see a British specialist after having spent large sums of money in a fruitless search for treatment for her limp left arm and lifeless leg back home in Pakistan.

Gulshan was the youngest daughter of a Muslim Sayed family, descended from the prophet Mohammed and brought up according to the strict orthodox Islamic code of the Shias. Her father and the whole family had prayed fervently to Allah for her healing, and now they waited anxiously on that April morning for Dr David to begin his examination. The room was filled with tension as he announced to Gulshan and her father, "There is no medicine for this – only prayer." There was no mistaking the firm finality in his voice. Even though she was distraught Gulshan was amazed to hear a western person speak about God. Her father told her that they must keep on praying and believing and that surely God would heal her as they pilgrimaged to Mecca for the Hajj in just a few days time.

During those days of waiting Gulshan had plenty of time to think about her future as a helpless cripple should she never be healed. Was she really destined to spend her days with withered limbs, with the skin turned black, wrinkled and hanging loose, and with whatever fingers there were sticking together like jelly? At an age when her peers dreamt of marriage and family here she was facing a lonely uncertain painful future, a non-person, never to be a whole, proper woman, behind a veil of shame.

When their plane touched down at the airport in Mecca they were met by a family friend, a Sheikh who was known for his kind and generous hospitality. He had eight wives and eighteen children living in his huge villa.

When they finally arrived at the Hajji -Camp, or pilgrims' rest, hundreds of thousands had began to gather in Mecca for the festival which every Muslim who was able was expected to attend at least once in their lifetime. It is one of the five pillars on which Islam is based. As the pilgrims walked or ran around the huge, cube-like, granite building known as the *Ka'aba*, the House of God, Gulshan was filled with excitement, surely she thought, "God would heal me here!" As they went around the *Ka'aba*, three times running, four walking, they passed the Black Stone on the north-east corner, said to have been put there by Mohammed with his own hands. The last time around they stopped at this stone which was also said to have been thrown down to Adam by God and was a powerful symbol of Islamic faith, touched by God, Adam and

Mohammed. Gulshan was helped to lean forward and kiss the stone which was now set in silver and sprayed with perfume. As she did so she prayed, “Please heal me, and heal these others.” But nothing happened. They next moved on to the praying place of Abraham and again she prayed to be healed and again nothing happened.

After several days many of the pilgrims went on to Medina, the second most important city for Muslims, 250 miles away, where Mohammed lived for ten years after he was driven from Mecca and where he set up Islam in 662. Gulshan visited the great Mosque at Madni and paid homage at Mohammed’s tomb but still no healing. From Medina they went on to Jerusalem and the Al-Masjid al-Agsa Mosque, towards which Mohammed prayed before Mecca became his centre. The Dome of the Rock is right next to it. Next they went on to Karbala in Iraq to see where the grandson of Mohammed, Hussein, and his family and servants were buried. They prayed for healing there also but still none was given. They were on pilgrimage for one month before they finally returned home to Karachi.

Two years later in December, 1968, Gulshan’s beloved father died as a result of pneumonia. Almost his last words to her were, “One day God is going to heal you, pray to Him.” Gulshan was overcome with grief and wanted to die. It was then out of sheer anguish and helplessness she began to call upon God and really talk to Him, not as a Muslim does using set prayers, approaching Him across a great gulf, but driven by a vast emptiness inside she prayed as if talking to one who knew all about her deepest pain and need.

“What terrible sin have I committed, that you have made me to live like this?” she sobbed. “As soon as I was born my mother was taken away, and then you made me a cripple, and now you’ve taken away my father. Tell me why have you punished me so heavily?”

Then she heard a low gentle voice in her own language, “I won’t let you die. I will keep you alive.” She felt a wonderful new freedom to commune with God.

“What’s the point of keeping me alive?” she queried. “I’m a cripple...you’ve taken away my father and left me with no hope, nothing to live for.”

She heard the same voice once more, “Who gave eyes to the blind, and who made the sick whole, and who healed the lepers and who raised the dead? I am Jesus, son of Mary. Read about me in the Koran, in the Sura Maryam.”

This began a study of the Koran for everything it had to say about Jesus. When she asked her aunty what she knew about Jesus, she was told matter of factly, “He’s the only prophet in the Holy Koran who gives eyes to the blind and who raises the dead and who is coming again.”

Gulshan said, “For years I had read the Holy Koran devotedly and prayed regularly, but I had lost all hope that my condition would change. Now, however, I began to believe that what was written about Jesus was true – that He did miracles, was alive – and that He could heal me. Oh Jesus son of Mary, it says in the Holy Koran that you have raised the dead and healed the lepers and done miracles, so heal me too.”

The more she prayed the more she was drawn closer to Jesus who had power that Mohammed himself never claimed. He never raised the dead or healed the sick.

Encounter with Jesus

It was 3am and Gulshan was sitting up in bed reading verses that she knew by heart about Jesus. But why was she still a cripple? Why was there still no answer to her cry for healing? She tells what happened next,

“I cried out in a fever of pain, ‘If you are able to, heal me – otherwise tell me’. What happened next is something I find hard to put into words. I know that the whole room filled with light. At first I thought it was from my reading lamp beside the bed, then I saw that its light looked dim. Perhaps it was the dawn? But it was too early for that. The light was growing, growing in brightness, until it surpassed the day. I covered myself with my shawl I was so frightened.

“Then the thought occurred to me that it might be the gardener who had switched on the light outside to shine on the trees. I came out from my shawl to look but the doors and windows were fast shut, with curtains and shutters drawn. I then became aware of figures in long robes, standing in the midst of the light, some feet from my bed. There were twelve figures in a row and the figure in the middle, the thirteenth, was larger and brighter than the others.

“‘Oh God’, I cried and the perspiration broke out on my forehead. I bowed my head and prayed, ‘Oh God, who are these people, and how have they come here when all the windows and doors are shut?’

“Suddenly a voice said, ‘Get up. This is the path you have been seeking. I am Jesus, son of Mary, to whom you have been praying, and now I am standing in front of you. You get up and come to me.’

“I started to weep, ‘Oh Jesus, I’m crippled. I can’t get up.’

“He said, ‘Stand up and come to me. I am Jesus.’

"When I hesitated He said it a second time. Then as I still doubted He said for the third time, 'Stand up.'

"And I, Gulshan Fatima, who had been crippled on my bed for nineteen years, felt new strength flowing into my wasted limbs. I put my foot on the ground and stood up. Then I ran a few paces and fell at the feet of the vision. I was bathing in the purest light, and it was burning as bright as the sun and the moon together. The light shone into my heart and into my mind and many things became clear to me at that moment.

"Jesus put His hand on the top of my head, and I saw a hole in His hand from which a ray of light struck down upon my garments, so that the green dress looked white.

"He said, 'I am Jesus. I am Immanuel. I am the Way, the Truth and the Life. I am alive, and I am coming soon. See, from today you are my witness. What you have now seen with your eyes you must take to my people.'

"He said, 'Now you have to keep this robe and your body spotless. Wherever you go I will be with you, and from today you must pray like this: "Our Father which art in heaven, hallowed be thy name. Thy kingdom come. Thy will be done, on earth as it is in heaven. Give us this day our daily bread, and forgive us our trespasses, as we forgive them that trespass against us, and lead us not into temptation but deliver us from evil: for thine is the kingdom and the power and the glory for ever and ever. Amen."'"

"He made me repeat the prayer, and it sank down into my heart and mind. It was beautiful in its simplicity, yet its profundity, so different from the prayers I had learned to say from my childhood. It called God 'Father' – that was a name that clutched at my heart, that filled its emptiness.

"I wanted to remain there at the feet of Jesus, praying this new name of God – 'Our Father'...but the Jesus vision had more to say to me, 'Read in the Koran, I am alive and coming soon.' This I had been taught and it gave me faith in what I was hearing. Jesus said much more. I was so full of joy. It could not be described.

"I looked at my arm and my leg. There was flesh on them. My hand was not perfect; nevertheless, it had strength and was no longer withered and wasted.

"'Why don't you make it all whole?'" I asked.

"The answer came lovingly: 'I want you to be my witness.'

"The figures were going up out of my sight and fading. I wanted Jesus to stay a little longer, and I cried out with sorrow. Then the light went and I found myself alone, standing in the middle of the room, wearing a white garment, and with my eyes heavy from the dazzling light. I groped towards a chest of drawers which stood against the wall. In them I found a pair of sunglasses, which I wore in the garden. I put them on and was able to comfortably open my eyes to see again.

"I carefully shut the drawer, then turned and looked around at my room. It was just the same as when I woke up. The clock still ticked on my bedside table, showing that it was almost 4am. The door was firmly shut and the windows, with the curtains drawn tightly across, were closed against the cold. I had not imagined the scene, however, for I had the evidence in my body. I took a few steps, then a few more. I walked from wall to wall, up and down, up and down. My limbs were unmistakably healthy on the side that had been paralyzed. Oh, the joy I felt. 'Father,' I cried. 'Our Father, which art in heaven.' It was a new and wonderful prayer.

"There was a knocking at the door. It was Aunty. 'Gulshan,' she said urgently. 'Who is in your room walking?' 'It's me Aunt,' I said.

"There was a little gasp and then my Aunt's voice, 'Oh, that's impossible. You can't be treated. How can you walk? You're telling lies.' 'Well come in and see,' I answered.

"The door opened slowly and Aunty came fearfully into the room. She stood pressed against the wall in terror and disbelief, her eyes wide open and staring at my radiant face. 'You'll fall,' she said. 'I won't fall,' I laughed, feeling the power and strength of new life coursing through my veins. My Aunt came forward slowly, hands outstretched, like a blind person feeling her way. She drew up the sleeve of my tunic and looked at my arm, plump and healthy as it had become. Then she asked me to sit on the bed and looked at my leg, which was as whole as the other.

"'It looks strange to seeing you stand. I have to get use to this,' she said.

"She asked me to tell her how it happened. So I told Aunty from the beginning, first about Father's prediction, then about the voice in my room on the night after he died. Then I told her about the three years of reading about Jesus in the Koran, ending with His appearance to me and my healing.

"When I got to the part about Jesus saying I was to be His witness, Aunt broke in with, 'There are no Christians in Pakistan for you to witness to and there's no need for you to go to America or England. Your witness should be to give alms to the poor. When these people come to you for food and money, that will be your witness.'

"I had not up to then connected the commission given me by Jesus with going to America or England. Yet His words were still real and present: 'What you have seen with your eyes you must take to my people. My people are your people.'"

Her Aunt's reaction was an indication of what was to come. First Gulshan became well known and famous. Her village and family were delighted with her healing but did not like all the talk about Jesus. They tried to persuade her to give the credit to Mohammed but she held firm in her testimony and told them that Jesus was 'The Way, the Truth and the Life.'

God supernaturally led her to a Christian couple near her village who gave her a Bible and it was not long after she was baptised proclaiming Jesus as her Lord and Saviour. This brought tremendous persecution from her family and she was immediately disowned and warned by her eldest brother, Safdar, that the Koran allowed him to kill his sister for what she had done and he would still go to paradise.

Some years later Safdar gave a gun to his younger brother, Alim, and told him to shoot their sister if she refused to deny her faith in Jesus. But she faithfully proclaimed Him and her brother was unable to pull the trigger.

She was cast out of her home, deprived of her inheritance and ostracized by her family but the joy of the Lord captivated her heart and radiated on her face as Jesus miraculously protected and provided for her even when she was thrown into prison for her beliefs. She saw her sister raised from the dead and come to trust Jesus for her salvation. She has been faithful to the commission Jesus gave her to be His witness having travelled throughout the world telling what He has done and is able to do in a person's life that is surrendered to Him. She has also written two books *The Torn Veil,* and *Beyond the Veil*, which have become best sellers.

Nineteen years after her encounter with Jesus she had a phone call from her younger brother, Alim, in 1990. He told her excitedly that he wanted her to come back to Pakistan as soon as she could, as he had some important news. She went immediately and recounts what happened when they met,

"Alim said that he had had a massive heart attack, his third, and was taken to the UCH Hospital in Lahore – an American hospital run by Christians. There he was pronounced dead, and his body was undressed and laid on a slab in an empty room. The doctor then locked the door while he completed all the paperwork, including the death certificate. His family were informed of his death and were asked to come and collect the body.

"Meanwhile my now dead brother found himself in a terrible place. He realised that it must be hell, because everyone seemed to be burning in a fire. Alim was in a corner and by this time was screaming and shouting for help. Then he noticed what looked like starlight, and in the middle of the light was a crowd of people who were worshipping a man they called Jesus, the Son of God. He recognised the name that I had spoken about so often. He then approached Jesus and said, 'Please, Jesus, you helped my sister Gulshan, please, help me. You are the only one who can get me out of this terrible place.'

"Then Jesus looked at Alim, and said, 'My son, leave this place and live for me.'

"Suddenly Alim woke up to find himself in a locked room, naked and lying on a slab. Eight hours had passed since he was pronounced dead. He got up, found his clothes in a cupboard, dressed, and then waited for someone to find him.

"When the houseboy, who had been told by the doctor to get the dead body to give to the family, saw Alim sitting up on the slab, he was terrified and quickly ran out of the room. News of what had happened spread like wildfire throughout the hospital, and when Alim's wife saw him, she fainted.

"Alim refused to leave the hospital until he was baptised in the chapel adjacent to the hospital. At first opportunity he told all my family that I was right about what I said about Jesus, and that they must change their attitude towards me, which they did. From that time on Alim was a faithful witness to Jesus until his sudden death seven years later. So, I am now reconciled with all my family, and when I go back to Pakistan I always receive a warm welcome, and they even ask me to pray for them in times of difficulty."

Healing Encounters

10

SMITH WIGGLESWORTH

Ever Increasing Faith

"The all important thing is to make Jesus Lord. Men can grow lopsided by emphasising the truth of divine healing. Men can get it wrong by all the time preaching water baptism. But we never go wrong in exalting the Lord Jesus Christ, giving Him the pre-eminent place and magnifying Him as both Lord and Christ, yes as very God of very God. As we are filled with the Spirit our one desire is to magnify Him. We need to be filled with the Spirit to get the full revelation of the Lord Jesus Christ."

Smith Wigglesworth became a legend even within his own lifetime. He was a plumber from Bradford, England, whom God took and used in a unique and amazing way. He lived and walked continually in the presence of God.

People born blind and deaf, cripples twisted and deformed by disease, others on death's door with cancer or sickness of every kind, all were healed by the mighty power of God through his ministry.

Born in 1859 into poverty, Smith Wigglesworth was converted through the Methodists at eight years of age. Even then, he was hungry for God and hungry for souls, and joined the choir of the local Episcopal church. "When most of the boys in the choir were twelve years of age they had to be confirmed by the bishop. I was not twelve, but between nine and ten, when the bishop laid his hands on me. I can remember that as he imposed his hands I had a similar experience to the one I had forty years later when I was baptized in the Holy Spirit. My whole body was filled with the consciousness of God's presence, a consciousness that remained with me for days. After the confirmation service all the other boys were swearing and quarrelling, and I wondered what had made the difference between them and me," he said.

Later, Wigglesworth was baptised by full immersion in water by the Baptists and had grounding in Bible teaching among the Plymouth Brethren. He also marched under the Blood and Fire banner of the Salvation Army, learning to win souls in the open air.

In 1907, when he was 48, his life was dramatically changed. From a relatively small, part-time ministry, God thrust him into a world-wide evangelistic ministry.

Many books have been written attempting to find the secret of Wigglesworth's power, but the answer is very simple. His great faith came from his relationship with Jesus Christ. From that relationship came Smith's every answer to every situation he ever faced.

The accounts of his life and ministry fill countless volumes and though his methods were sometimes unorthodox they were incredibly effective. Here are just a couple of the thousands of incidents he recalls,

"My friend said, 'She is dead.' He was scared. I have never seen a man so frightened in my life. 'What shall I do?' he asked. You may think that what I did was absurd, but I reached over into the bed and pulled her out. I carried her across the room, stood her against the wall and held her up, as she was absolutely dead. I looked into her face and said, 'In the name of Jesus, I rebuke this death.' From the crown of her head to the soles of her feet her whole body began to tremble. 'In the name of Jesus, I command you to walk,' I said. I repeated, 'In the name of Jesus, in the name of Jesus, walk!' and she walked."

Jesus' Smile

The wife of a devoted friend was so ill that the doctors expected her to die during the night. Smith's friend said he couldn't believe for his wife, because he didn't know how. Compassion rose up in Smith's heart and he determined to help the family, so he went to a minister who was opening a small church in Bradford, and asked if he would go to pray for the woman. The minister refused however. Smith then went to a friend, who agreed to go with him, and the two set out for the woman's home.

Smith felt encouraged to have someone with him. He exhorted his friend to begin praying as soon as they entered the home, and upon seeing the weakened condition of the woman, the friend took Smith's advice. He began praying but not as Smith had hoped. This man prayed for the family that would be left behind and continued in a rambling, negative

tone until Smith cried out for him to stop. Thinking the worst was behind him, he then asked the woman's husband to pray. But he cried out in just as pathetic a fashion. Finally, when Smith could stand it no longer, he cried out so loudly that he could be heard in the street – "Lord, stop him!" The husband stopped.

Smith then pulled a bottle of oil out of his pocket and poured the entire bottle over the body of the woman. Then at the head of her bed, Smith saw Jesus standing there. He said, "Suddenly the Lord Jesus appeared. I had my eyes open gazing at Him. He gave me one of those gentle smiles. I have never lost that vision, the vision of that beautiful, soft smile." A few moments later the vision vanished, and the woman sat up in bed filled with new life. She lived to raise a number of children and outlived her husband.

Jesus' Beauty

"I was in Havre in France and the power of God was being mightily manifested," Wigglesworth recounted. "A Greek man named Felix attended the meetings and became very zealous for God. He was very anxious to get all the Catholics he could to the meeting in order that they should see that God was graciously visiting France. He found a certain bed-ridden woman who was fixed in a certain position and could not move, and he told her about the Lord healing at the meetings and that he would get me to come if she wished. She said, 'My husband is a Catholic and he would never allow anyone who was not a Catholic to see me.'

"She asked her husband to allow me to come and told him what Felix had told her about the power of God working in our midst. He said, 'I will have no Protestant enter my house.' She said, 'You know the doctors cannot help me, and the priests cannot help, won't you let this man of God pray for me?' He finally consented and I went to the house. The simplicity of this woman and her child-like faith were beautiful to see.

"I showed her my oil bottle and said to her, 'Here is oil. It is a symbol of the Holy Ghost. When that comes upon you, the Holy Ghost will begin to work, and the Lord will raise you up.' And God did something the moment the oil fell upon her. I looked toward the window and I saw Jesus. (I have seen Him often. There is no painting that is a bit like Him, no artist can ever depict the beauty of my lovely Lord.) The woman felt the power of God in her body and cried, 'I'm free, my hands are free, my shoulders are free, and oh, I see Jesus! I'm free! I'm free!'

"The vision vanished and the woman sat up in bed. Her legs were still bound, and I said to her, 'I'll put my hands over your legs and you will be free entirely.' And as I put my hands on those legs covered with bed clothes, I looked and saw the Lord again. She saw Him too and cried, 'He's there again. I'm free! I'm free!' She rose from her bed and walked round the room praising God, and we were all in tears as we saw His wonderful works."

11

BETTY BAXTER

A Remarkable Healing

The healing of Betty Baxter is one of the most amazing I have ever come across. I first heard her testimony more than twenty five years ago and was thrilled to discover more details through my research.

There is a Betty Baxter website where you can hear her personal testimony. I have also included as an appendix the newspaper article from the *Fairmount Sentinel* which was the first newspaper to run the incredible story.

Betty's Story

"As far back as I can remember I wasn't normal like other boys and girls. My body was twisted and crippled and deformed. I guess I will never forget that awful feeling of no hope. I know how it feels to have the family doctor look in my face and say, 'Betty, there is no hope.' Also to be carried from one hospital to another and see the specialists shake their heads and say, 'There is nothing medical science can do.'

"I was born with a curve in my spine. Every vertebra was out of place. As you know the nerves are centred on the spine. The X-rays showed that the bones were twisted and matted together; therefore my nervous system was wrecked.

"One day as I lay in the University Hospital in Minneapolis, Minnesota, I began to shake all over. It was sort of a trembling at first but soon I was shaking violently from head to toe. I shook out of my bed and fell on the floor. The doctor rushed in and put me back on the bed. He said, 'This is what I have been expecting. She now has St Vitus Dance and there is nothing to do but send her home.'

"They took wide straps and strapped my body to the bed. It didn't keep me from shaking but it did keep me from falling out of bed. They kept me strapped to the bed day and night, only removing them long enough for my nurse to bathe me. When the straps were removed my body would be raw and blistered.

"I know what it is to suffer. I lived in pain. The doctors kept me on drugs so I could endure the pain. When I came into the world my heart was not normal and under the power of the drugs it grew worse. Eventually I came to have a heart attack about every week.

"At last my body became so accustomed to the medication that it couldn't take full effect. I would bite my lips to keep from screaming while the hypo took effect and then, when the pain would not go, I would scream for another injection. Only after two or three injections could I get any relief from the torturing racking pain.

“I remember the day the doctor took me off dope. He said to mom, ‘Mrs Baxter, it isn’t doing her any good. Her body is accustomed to it.’ He removed everything from my bed and said, ‘Betty, I’m sorry but I can’t keep giving you morphine injections.’ I was only nine-years-old at that time. Oh how long the nights were as I lay racked with pain. Many times I would twist in the bed struggling for a little relief and feel myself blacking out. Then for hours I would lay unconscious.

“I was raised in a Christian home. Mom had taught me ever since I can remember the story of Jesus. My mother believed the Bible and told me that Jesus was the same Saviour today as He was when He walked the sandy shores of Galilee and that He still heals today if people will only believe and have faith in Him.

“Before I go further into my story I want to say that the greatest miracle that ever took place in my life was not when Jesus healed my crippled, twisted, deformed body but when He saved my soul from sin. As long as I had Jesus in my heart, I could go to heaven even though I was crippled and deformed.

“My conversion happened when I was only nine years old after hearing our pastor, Brother Davis, tell what he said was the ‘Greatest Story in the World.’ Beginning at Jesus’ birth, he told the beautiful story, finally ending with the cross and the resurrection. He told how with His two precious hands He touched the blind eyes and they saw; how He touched the deaf ear and it was unstopped; how He cleansed the leper, how He fed the multitude with a little boy’s lunch; how His feet carried Him over the hot blistering sands of Galilee while He preached the gospel to the people; how He walked on the water and did not sink. He told how the people, after all this, took Jesus and pierced His two precious hands with nails, and thrust a spear in His side and when they pulled it out, blood and water gushed out of His side and flowed down His limbs, the royal blood spilling on the ground. He said this blood had power to save from sin and heal our bodies from affliction today. It was the best story I had ever heard. Tears began trickling down my cheeks. I found myself kneeling and asking Jesus to save me.

"I told Brother Davis I was going to be an evangelist. Then he gently put his hand on my head and prayed a blessing over me. Later he told my parents 'Don't ever let this girl get away from the call of God. I have never seen a child her age have such an experience with the Lord as she has.'

"But the hand of affliction began to cut my life short. The only relief I got was through my mother's prayers. My daddy did not have the faith in Jesus to heal my body as Mom did but he was a good dad to me and never hindered Mom from praying for me. My mother loved Jesus with a great love. I believe she understood Jesus better than anyone I ever knew. She seemed to know how to make my faith grow in Jesus for Him to heal me someday.

"My darkest hour came while they were wheeling me down the hospital corridor on a stretcher. The doctor walked up, stopped the stretcher, looked down at me and said, 'Betty, we have X-rayed your spine. Every vertebra is out of place; the bones are twisted and matted together. Also you need a new kidney; as long as the old kidney remains you will have pain.'

"'Well, Mr Baxter,' the doctor said, 'We can never hope to untangle that mass of bones in Betty's body. Take her home and let her be as happy as possible.' I was eleven-years-old at that time and had no idea that the doctor was sending me home to die. I looked at him, 'Yes, Doctor, but someday God will heal my body. I will be well and strong then.'

"I had faith then for Mom had read God's word to me and talked to me about Jesus so that my faith was strong. One of Mom's favourite Scriptures in those days was, *'If thou canst believe all things are possible to him that believeth.'* Also, *'Nothing is impossible with God.'*

"They took me home where the doctor said I would soon die. I grew worse. The pain I had suffered before was nothing compared to what I began to feel after I returned home. I would go blind and for weeks could not see; I would become deaf and could not hear; dumb and could not speak. My tongue would swell and then would be paralyzed. Then the blindness would leave, also the deafness and paralysis of the tongue. It seemed I was caught; some awful power was trying to destroy me. But each day Mom would pray with me and tell me God was able to heal my body.

"As I lay there during those years of loneliness, isolated from the world, I found out one thing: Jesus had promised, *'I will never leave you nor forsake you.'* So it was during those years of loneliness that I got acquainted with the King of Kings and Lord of Lords. Many people have said, 'Betty, why didn't God heal you when you were a little child and had such great faith?' I don't know. God's ways are not my ways. God's ways are best. There is one thing I do know during those awful years of loneliness and pain, I really got to know Jesus.

"Mom would bathe me in the mornings and then she would leave me. Sometimes I would hear a soft walk by my bedside and would wonder if Mom had come in the room while I was not listening. Then I would hear a soft voice that I learned to know. It was not Dad's voice. It was not Mom's voice. It was not my doctor's voice. It was Jesus speaking to me.

The First Encounter

"The first time this happened He called me by my first name three times, very softly. 'Betty!' 'Betty!' 'Betty!' He called me three times before I answered. I said, 'Yes, Lord, stay and talk with me for a little while because I am so lonesome.' Would He stay and talk with me? Yes, He would. He said a lot of things but one thing I will never forget. I believe the reason He always told me this was because He knew it thrilled me most. This is what He always said, 'Betty, I love you!' Jesus would look down upon me in my pitiful condition so crippled and deformed that when my daddy would stand me up I stood only as high as my little four-year-old brother. Large knots had grown on my spine, the first one at the base of my neck, then one right after the other to the base of my spine. My arms were paralyzed from my shoulders to my wrists. I could only move my fingers. My head was twisted and turned down on my chest. When I drank water I had to drink from a tube because I couldn't raise my head. Yet in this condition Jesus whispered that He loved me. I said, 'Jesus, help me to be patient because I can do anything as long as I know you love me!' Many times He whispered, 'Remember child, I will never leave you nor forsake you.'

"Listen friend, I am confident that He loved me just as much when I was crippled, forgotten by all the world, as He does right now when I am well and strong and able to work for Him. I remember as Jesus stood by my bedside I would ask Him, 'Jesus, do you know the doctors won't give me any morphine for my pain? I wonder if you know how sharp that pain is in my back where the knots are.' And Jesus would say, 'Oh, yes, I know. Don't you remember? One day when I hung between heaven and earth I took the pain and sickness of the whole world upon me there.'

"As the years went by I gave up all hope of ever being made well by a doctor. Finally, my dad came in and took my crippled body in his arms and sat on the edge of his bed. He looked at me with big tears splashing down his rugged face. He said, 'Honey, you don't know, you don't have the least idea what money is but I have given up everything, I have spent all

I have and more too in order to get you well. Betty, your daddy has gone as far as he can go. There isn't any hope anymore.' He took out his handkerchief and wiped his face dry. Then looking at me he said, 'I don't believe Jesus will let you suffer much longer. He's going to take you to that place called heaven and when you get inside stand there and watch everyone that enters. Someday you will see daddy coming through those gates. It won't be long. The doctors say it will be soon.'

"I want to say right here that although I had given up hope as far as man's help is concerned, I still had faith in God. One day just before the sun went down I was struck with such unbearable pain that I lapsed into unconsciousness. Three hours later, my mother noticed my breathing was too slow and I scarcely had any pulse. She called the doctor. After an examination, he said, 'This is the end. She will never regain consciousness.' I lay unconscious for four days and nights. The family was called in and they took up the death-watch.

"The fifth morning I remember opening my eyes. Mom leaned over the bed and put her cool hand on my burning forehead. I felt as if I was burning up inside. Knife-like pains were shooting through my spine. Mother said, 'Betty, it's Mother, don't you know me?' I couldn't speak but smiled at her. She raised her hands toward heaven and began praising God for she felt God had answered her prayers and given me back to her. As I lay there looking at her, I thought, 'which would I rather do – stay here with my mother and daddy or go to that place mother has read to me about, a place where there is no pain?'

"I prayed a prayer that day that I suppose many other people have prayed. 'Jesus, I know that I am saved and am ready to go to heaven. Now Lord, all these years I have prayed to be healed but I have been denied. Lord, I have reached the end of the way and I'm not particular what you do. Please come and take me to that place called heaven.' As I prayed a thick darkness settled over me. I felt coldness creeping through my body. In a moment's time, it seemed, I was cold all over and completely surrounded by darkness. As a child I had always been afraid of the dark so I began crying, 'Where am I? What is this place? Where is my daddy? I want my daddy.'

"As the darkness settled about me, I saw through the darkness a long, dark, narrow valley. I went inside this valley. I began to scream, 'Where am I? What is this place?' and from a distance I recognized my mother's voice speaking slowly, *'Yea though I walk through the valley of the shadow of death, I will fear no evil for thou art with me.'*

"I remember saying, 'This must be the valley of death. I prayed to die and I guess to get to Jesus I will have to walk it,' and I started through this dark place. I had barely got inside when the place lit up with the light of day. I felt something strong and firm take hold of my hand. I didn't need to look. I knew it was the strong and nail-scarred hand of the Son of God who had saved my soul. He took my hand and held it tightly and I went on through the valley. I wasn't afraid anymore. I was happy for now I was going home. My mother had said in heaven I would have a new body, one that would be straight instead of bent and twisted and crippled.

"At last we heard music in the distance, the most beautiful music I ever heard. We quickened our steps. We came to a wide river separating us from that beautiful land. I looked on the other side and saw green grass, flowers of every colour, beautiful flowers that would never die. I saw the river of life winding its way through the city of God. Standing on its banks was a company of those who had been redeemed by the blood of the Lamb and they were singing, 'Hosanna to the King.' I looked at them, not a single one had knots on their spine or a face marred and marked with pain. I said, 'In a few minutes I'm going to join that heavenly band and the moment I step on the other side I will straighten up and be well and strong.'

“I was anxious to get across. I knew I wouldn’t have to cross it alone for Jesus would be with me. But at that very moment I heard the voice of Jesus and I stood to attention as I do when I hear the Master’s voice. Very softly and with great kindness Jesus said, ‘No, Betty, it’s not your time to cross yet. Go back and fulfill the call I gave you when you were nine years old. Go back for you are going to have healing in the autumn.’

“As I stood and listened to the words of Jesus, I must confess I was disappointed. I remember I said, as tears rolled down my face, ‘When I’m so close to happiness and health why must Jesus deny me? I’ve never known a well day in my life, now when I’m so close to heaven, why can’t I go on in?’

“Then I thought, ‘Oh, what am I saying?’ Turning to Jesus I said, ‘Lord, I’m sorry. Your way is better than my way. I’ll go back.’ I slowly regained consciousness. Then the doctor said I would not last through the summer months. For weeks after that I could not speak. The knots grew larger. I would hear Mom say, ‘Dad, look, the knots are so hard and they are getting larger. She must be suffering.’

“Early summer came. Everyone in Martin County, Minnesota, knew the little Baxter girl was dying. Saints and sinners alike came to my bedside but most of the time I was unconscious. When I was conscious they would pat me on the shoulder, say a kind word, and pass on. I never gave up hope. I couldn’t speak out loud but in my heart I said, ‘Lord, as soon as Autumn comes I’ll have healing, won’t I Jesus?’ I never doubted because Jesus never breaks a promise. He was going to heal me in the autumn.

“That summer, on the 14th day of August, my speech returned. I hadn’t spoken for weeks and I said, ‘Mom, what day is today?’ She said, ‘The 14th day of August.’ My daddy came in at noon. I said, ‘Daddy, where’s the big chair? Please put the pillows in it and set me in the big chair.’ The only way I could sit in the chair was with my head resting on my knees and my arms hanging down at my sides. I said, 'Daddy, when you go out close the door. Tell Mom not to come in for a while, I want to be alone.' I heard my daddy sob as he left the room and he didn't ask any questions. He knew why I wanted to be alone. I had an appointment with the King.

"I heard Dad click the door. I began to cry and sob. I didn't know how to pray. All I knew to do was merely talk to Jesus but it got the job done. I said, 'Lord, you remember months ago I almost got to heaven and you wouldn't let me in. Jesus, you promised if I would go back that you would have healing for me in the Fall (Autumn). I asked Mom this morning what day it was and she said the 14th day of August. Jesus, I guess you don't count this Fall yet because it's still awful hot but Lord, I wonder if just for this one year you could call this Fall and come and heal me? The pain is so bad, Jesus, I have gone as far as I can go. I can't stand the pain any longer. I wonder Lord if you will call this Fall and come and heal me?'

"I listened. Heaven was quiet. But I didn't give up. I began to cry again. I said, 'Lord, I'll tell you what I'll do. I'll make a bargain. Now Jesus, listen to me. I'm going to bargain with you. Jesus, if you will only heal me and make me well inside and outside I'll go out and preach every night until I'm ninety years old if you want me to.' I listened after I made these vows. This time I was rewarded. I heard the voice of Jesus speaking audibly to me. He spoke these words, **'I am going to heal you completely on August 24th, Sunday afternoon at three o'clock.'**

"A thrill of hope and expectancy swept through my entire body and soul. God told me the day and the hour. The first thought that came to me was, 'Won't Mom be glad when I tell her. Just think how happy she will be when I tell her. Just think how happy she will be when I tell her I know the day and the hour.' Then Jesus spoke again and said to me, 'Now, don't tell this until my time comes.'

"After Jesus told me this I felt like a new person. I didn't mind the sharp pains any more or the violent throbbing of my enlarged heart. The 24th day of August would soon come and I would have relief. I heard the door open and Mom walked in. She knelt down on the rug and looked up in my face. I wanted to tell her what Jesus had told me. The hardest thing I ever did was to keep from telling her.

"I looked at Mom. I thought, 'Something has happened to Mom, she looks so pretty and young today.' Then I thought the reason she looked so different was that I knew the secret about my healing next Sunday. I looked at her again and I was convinced more than ever that something had happened to her. Her eyes had never shone like that before. Then all at once she leaned over me, pushed the hair back from my forehead and said, 'Honey, do you know when the Lord is going to heal you?' Oh, I knew but I wasn't supposed to tell. I couldn't say 'No,' for I would not be telling the truth. So I said,

'When?'

"Mom smiled and said, 'August 24th, Sunday afternoon at three o'clock.'

"I said, 'Mom, how did you know? Did I let it slip and tell you?'

"She said, 'No, the same God that talks to you talks to me.'

"When my mother said that I was doubly sure God would heal my body the 24th day of August and make me well. I said, 'Mom, am I getting straighter? Are the knots going away?' She looked at me and said, 'No, Betty, you are getting more bent every day and the knots are growing larger.'

"I said, 'Mom, do you still believe God will heal me the 24th day of August?'

"She said, 'Sure I do. All things are possible if we only believe.'

"Many people have asked how my mother knew the day I would be healed. While the Lord was talking to me the rest of the family was in the dining room eating. My mother had taken a fork full of food and as she was about to put it into her mouth it dropped back on the plate with a clatter. Then she heard the inner voice of God speak and say, 'I have heard your prayers and I am going to reward you for your faithfulness. I am going to heal Betty, August 24th Sunday afternoon at three o'clock, and she knows the same thing, as I have already told her.'

A New Dress

"I said, 'Mom, listen to me. I haven't had a dress on or shoes on my feet since I was a little girl. I have worn these night clothes all these years. Mom, when Jesus heals me Sunday afternoon I'm going to church Sunday night. The stores are closed on Sunday. Mom, if you really believe Jesus is going to heal me, will you go to Fairmont this afternoon and get me some new clothes? Will you, Mom?' 'Sure, I will go into town today and get you some clothes so you can wear them Sunday night,' she said.

"As she was driving away, Dad stopped her. 'Where are you going?' 'I'm going to town,' she said. 'What for?' he asked. 'Well, I am going to get a new dress and shoes for Betty,' she said. 'Now, Mother, you know we won't have to buy her a new dress until we lay her away and let's not think about it until we have to,' Dad said. 'Oh, no, she has had word from Jesus that He is going to heal her Sunday afternoon, the 24th and I've had word too. I'm going to Fairmont to get some new clothes for her.' My mother brought them home and showed them to me. I thought the dress was the most beautiful I had ever seen. The shoes were patent leather and they were pretty.

"When people came to see me I would say, 'Mom, get my dress and shoes out and let my friends see them.' They looked at me, then at the dress and shoes, then at my mother. I knew they thought strange of me but I knew exactly what was going to happen the 24th day of August.

"Saturday the 23rd of August came. My mother always slept in a bed in my room so as to be near me. That night when she got me all settled I fell asleep. Sometime in the night I awakened. The moon was shining through the window across the foot of my bed. I heard somebody mumbling and I wondered if Daddy was in my room talking to my mother. Then I saw a form on bended knees with arms raised in the moonlight. It was Mom and tears were streaming down her face. She was praying, 'Lord Jesus, I've tried to be a good mother to Betty. I've tried hard to teach her about you. Now Jesus, I've never been away from her but when you heal her I'm going to let her go anywhere you want her to go, even across the stormy sea, because you are going to do for her tomorrow what no one else could ever do. She's yours, Jesus. Tomorrow is the day. You will set her free, won't you Jesus?' I dropped off to sleep again. I couldn't stay up to pray but Mom took my place. It is because of her faith that I believe in God today, that I have healing for my body.

"Sunday morning came. Daddy took my brothers and sisters to Sunday School. They said he requested prayer for me with a broken heart, telling the people that I was much worse and was going to die if God didn't undertake. I asked my pastor to be present that day at three o'clock but he said that he had an appointment to try out for a church in Chicago and that was the only time he could go but for us to wire him if I got my healing. My mother invited a few friends in, saying, 'Be sure and get here about 2.30 because three o'clock is the hour.'

"They came at two o'clock. They said, 'Mrs Baxter, we are early but we know something is going to happen and we don't want to miss it.' That is the atmosphere they had around me when I was healed. At fifteen minutes to three my mother came to my bedside. I said, 'Mom, what time is it?' She said, 'Just 15 minutes before Jesus is coming to heal you.'

"I said, 'Mom, take me in and place me in the big chair.' She carried me in and set my twisted body in the chair and propped me up with pillows. I saw the people as they knelt on the floor around my chair. I saw my baby brother, four years old, and I realized I was so bent that I stood only as high as he did. He knelt down by me, looked up and said, 'Sis, it's not very long now until you will be taller than me.'

"At ten minutes to three my mother asked me what I wanted them to do. I said, 'Mom, start praying, I want to be praying when Jesus comes.' I heard her sobbing and praying for Jesus to keep His promise and come and heal my body.

Jesus Came

"I didn't lose consciousness but I became lost in the Spirit of God. I saw before me two rows of trees, standing tall and straight. As I watched, I saw one of them in the centre begin to bend until the tip of it touched the ground. I wondered why this one tree was all bent over. Then down the road I saw Jesus. He came walking through the trees and my heart thrilled as it always does when I see Jesus. He came and stood by the bent tree. He stood and looked at it a moment and I wondered what He would do. Then looking at me He smiled and placed His hand on the bent tree. With a loud crack and pop it straightened up like the others. I said, 'That's me alright. He will touch my body and the bones will crack and pop and I will stand up straight and be well.'

"Suddenly, I heard a great noise as if a storm was coming up. I heard the wind as it roared. I tried to speak above the noise. 'He's coming. Don't you hear Him? He has come at last.' Then all at once the noise subsided. All was calm and quiet and I knew in this quietness Jesus would come. I sat in the big chair, a hopeless cripple. I was so hungry to see Him. All at once I saw a great, white, fleecy cloud form. It wasn't the cloud I was waiting for. Then out of the cloud stepped Jesus. It wasn't a vision, it wasn't a dream. I saw Jesus. As He came walking slowly toward me I looked on His face. The most striking thing about Jesus is His eyes. He was tall and broad and was dressed in robes glistening white. His hair was brown and parted in the middle. It fell over His shoulders in soft waves. I will never forget His eyes. Many times, when my body is worn and I'm asked to do something for Jesus I would like to say no. When I remember His eyes they compel me to go out into the harvest fields to win more souls.

"Jesus came slowly toward me with His arms outstretched toward me. I noticed the ugly prints of the nails in His hands. The closer He got to me the better I felt. When He came real close I began to feel very small and unworthy. I wasn't anything but a little forgotten girl who was deformed and crippled. Then all at once He smiled at me and I wasn't afraid anymore. He was my Jesus. His eyes held mine and if I ever looked into eyes filled with beauty and compassion, they were the eyes of Jesus. There aren't many people I've seen who have eyes like Jesus. When I see one who has that love and compassion in their eyes I wish I could just stay close to them. That is the way I feel about Jesus; I want to live as close to Him as I can.

"Jesus came and stood at the side of my chair. One part of His garment was loose and it fell inside my chair and if my arms had not been paralyzed I could have touched His garment. I had thought when He came to heal me I would start talking to Him and ask Him to heal me. But I couldn't say a word. I just looked at Him and kept my eyes on His dear face trying to tell Him how much I needed Him. He leaned down and looked up in my face and spoke softly. I can hear every word right now because it is written in my heart. He said very softly, 'Betty, you have been patient, kind and loving.' As He spoke these words I thought I could suffer 15 more years if I could see Jesus and hear Him speak to me again. He said, 'I am going to promise you health, joy and happiness.' I saw Him reach out His hand and I waited. Then I felt His hand go over the knots on my spine. People say, 'Don't you ever get tired of telling of your healing?' No, because every time I tell it I can feel His hand again.

"He placed His hand on the very centre of my spine on one of the large knots. All at once a hot feeling as hot as fire surged through my body. Two hot hands took my heart and squeezed it and when those hot hands let my heart go, I could breathe normal for the first time in my life. Two hot hands rubbed over the organs of my stomach and I knew my organic trouble was healed, I would not need a new kidney and I would be able to digest my food because He had healed me. The hot feeling ran on through my body. Then I looked at Jesus to see if He would leave me just healed inside. Jesus smiled and I felt the pressure of His hands on the knots and as His hands pressed in the middle of my spine there was a tingling sensation like I had touched a live wire. I felt

this sensation like an electrical current and stood on my feet totally straight – I was healed inside and outside. In ten seconds Jesus had healed me and made me every whit whole. He did for me in a few moments what the doctors on this earth could not do. The Great Physician did it and He did it perfectly.

"You say, 'Betty, how did you feel when you jumped out of the chair?' You'll never know unless you once were a hopeless cripple. You'll never know unless you sat in a chair with no hope. I ran to my mother and said, 'Mom, feel, are the knots gone?' She felt up and down my spine and said, 'Yes, they are gone! I heard the bones crack and pop. Betty, you're healed! You're healed! Praise Him for it!'

"I turned around and looked back at the chair that was empty and tears rolled down my cheeks. My body felt light all over because I didn't have any pain and I had always had pain. I felt tall because I had been bent almost double with my head on my chest, the knots were gone and my spine was straight. I raised my arms and pinched one of them. My arms had feeling. They weren't paralyzed anymore. Then I looked and saw my baby brother standing in front of the chair. Big tears were rolling down his little cheeks. Looking up at me I heard him say, 'I saw Sis jump out of the big chair. I saw Jesus heal Sis.' He was really thrilled. I picked up the chair, raised it above my head and said, 'See what the God I serve can do!'

"Standing right behind my baby brother Jesus still stood. He looked at me from the soles of my feet to the top of my head. I was straight and normal.

Holding my eyes with His, He began to speak slowly. He said. 'Betty, I am giving you the desire of your heart to be healed. You are normal and well. You have health now. You are completely well because I healed you.'"

Betty Baxter was true to her promise to serve and testify for Jesus. She has taken His word all over the world and now well into her eighties she is still ministering and telling her story.

Personal testimonies of those who were eye witnesses to Betty Baxter's healing that Sunday afternoon, August 24th, at the Baxter Farm Home near Granada, Minnesota.

I was there at the Baxter home when Betty was healed, and saw her healed with my own eyes. I knew her before she was healed. I saw how she suffered and how helpless and crippled she was, how she was made well and strong as any normal girl, and is well and strong today. Betty asked me one day before she was healed if I would testify for her when she was healed. I promised her I would. Betty was healed by the hand of God who undertook for her in answer to prayer.

George Sturm, Granada, Minnesota

I am sure that nothing I could say would add to Betty's testimony except that I know the story she tells is true. I was in their home many times, both before and after Betty was healed. I know how sick she was. I saw her crippled up just as she describes herself. Especially do I remember the time she sent for me to come, about two days before she was healed. It was almost like a little visit in heaven. She told me that she was to be healed and asked George, my husband, and me to be there. She set the time for us to come (2.30pm the following Sunday).

I have since heard Betty give her testimony many times and each time I have been unable to keep back the tears, as I remember how the whole family was under such a burden because of Betty's condition, as well as the terrible suffering of Betty herself. The Baxter's are just common people, and what God has done for them He will do for all who will humble themselves and seek Him with believing hearts.

Mrs George Sturm, Granada, Minnesota

My personal testimony regarding my daughter Betty's healing. It is a day I shall never forget. It was August 24th, when our wonderful Saviour touched Betty's afflicted body and completely healed her that Sunday afternoon. As we knelt to pray the mighty power of God came upon us. From then on I hardly knew what was happening. I rose to my feet and was standing praising God even before Betty was healed that afternoon, and I was fully expecting her healing then. The Lord has given Betty a wonderful privilege of telling the gospel story to thousands of how Jesus can save from all sin and heal today as He did at the beginning of the church and Christian era. We know that 'Jesus is the same yesterday, today, and forever.' Praise His Holy Name.

Testimony of Betty's mother, Mrs William Baxter

While praying for Betty Baxter's healing, before this particular time, I was assured that she would be healed, and that she would be an evangelist. I did not know just when, but as I drove over to the Baxter home that Sunday afternoon, August 24th, I prayed earnestly that God would give me the assurance about when she would be healed. The answer came to me that Betty would be healed that afternoon. I expected it to happen.

Something happened which I did not expect. I will tell what it was further on in my testimony.

As the friends gathered in it seemed as though everyone was waiting for something to come or happen. As the hour drew near, Betty asked for a drink of water. Her sister, Wanda, brought her a glass of water with a drinking tube, for Betty could not raise her head enough to drink from the glass without a tube. She sat in a chair with her head resting on her knee.

It was now nearing the hour for the fulfillment of the promise which Betty had been assured of her healing. Mrs Baxter said, “It is time for us to pray.” Betty was still sitting in the large chair. Wanda, Betty’s sister, and her aunt, Mrs Earl Adams, knelt on one side of the chair and Mrs Baxter and I knelt on the other side. Mrs Baxter asked me to lead in prayer. I prayed a short prayer, as it seemed to me there wasn’t much for me to say. Mrs Baxter asked Betty if she wanted to pray. She did not answer nor did she pray. Her mother asked a second time if she wanted to pray. Still no answer. I thought that was very strange. I looked up at Betty, and she seemed to be looking at something. The south door of the room was opened, and all at once something like a gust of wind filled the room. Then Betty said, “Oh, I see Jesus coming!” Then He went on to heal her. Then, all of a sudden she sprang to her feet, raised her arms above her head, and shouted, “He healed me! He healed me!” Then with her arms which only a minute before were both paralyzed, she picked up one of the dining chairs, raised it above her head and shouted, “See what my God can do for me!”

Now I will tell you what happened to me, which I did not expect. I expected to see Betty Baxter healed, but did not expect what happened to me. When I laid my hands upon

Betty the power of God which touched her and healed her, also fell upon me. There are no words which can express or explain it. It was the most wonderful experience I ever had. I never was demonstrative, as all my friends know, but it seemed that my very body would burst if I did not give vent to my feelings some way!

Dear friends, I believe this was only a little taste of what the saints of the Lord shall experience when they come face to face with our blessed Redeemer. Oh, what God would do for His people if they would only let Him have His way in their lives!

I have told many people about Betty's healing and my experience, and it has been a blessing to both saint and sinner. May this testimony be the means of many believing on the Lord Jesus Christ for their salvation and for their healing.

Testimony of Mrs George Teubner, Betty Baxter's Sunday School teacher.

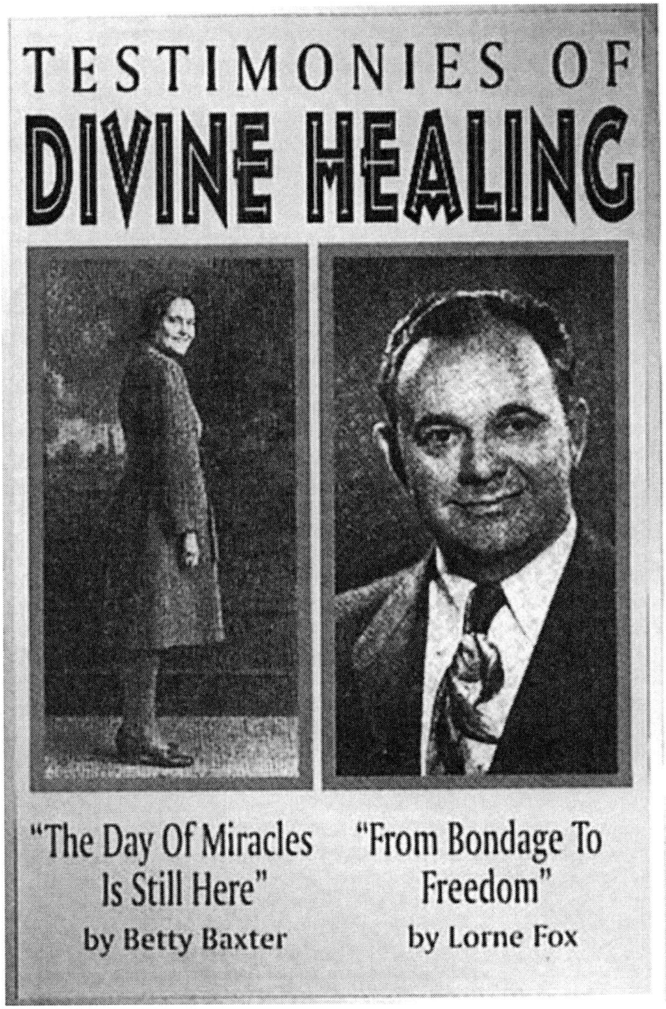
TESTIMONIES OF
DIVINE HEALING
"The Day Of Miracles Is Still Here"
by Betty Baxter
"From Bondage To Freedom"
by Lorne Fox

12

MIRACLES OF HEALING

Amelia

In over 50 years of her ministry, Kathryn Kuhlman witnessed to her Lord's love and power before more than 100,000,000 people. She is one of the most famous women evangelists of all time. She held miracle services all over the world but her base was in Carnegie Hall, Pittsburgh, USA, where she regularly filled the 7,000 seater auditorium and the meetings ran for over 20 years. It was at one of those services that a young child referred to by Miss Kuhlman as Amelia received an amazing miracle and says she saw Jesus standing on the platform next to the evangelist.

The story is told in Kathryn's Kuhlman's book, *I believe in Miracles* and I will let her tell exactly what happened,

"Little Amelia woke one morning with what appeared to be patches of a wet rash on her arms and legs. Before the week was out, her entire body was covered in running sores. As the days went on the sores began to bleed badly, and her whole body had to be encased in cloths. No water could touch her, and she was cleansed as gently as possible with oils. She was a pitiful sight with her arms wrapped in bandages and unable to bend them, they hung straight at the child's side. As her grandmother said, her whole skin was cracked open, blood and pus constantly oozed out. She was in continual pain, and it was torture for her to have her dressings changed. She screamed if anyone came near her. She was examined by doctor after doctor but they disagreed on her diagnosis, but were in unanimous agreement on one point; whatever the disease was, it was the worst skin ailment they had ever encountered in their practice of medicine.

"Finally, one of the physicians suggested that Amelia be taken to the cancer clinic and arrangements were made. But before this took place the child's grandmother asked permission to take her grand-daughter to the miracle services in Pittsburgh. Amelia's mother not only agreed but said she would pray at home during the hours of the service the following day.

"When I asked my son to drive us to the service, the grandmother said, he hesitated, 'You can't possibly take her into a crowd of people, looking as she does,' he said. By now it was impossible to comb her hair, so covered with sores was her scalp. She had no eyebrows left and even her eyelids were eaten away with sores. Her ears were actually rotting away and one ear seemed literally to be hanging off. Her face and little body had become equally ravaged. Other children were not allowed to play with her and people avoided her when she was out in public. She would often cry and say to her mother, 'Why doesn't anyone like me?' until the day came that she was a prisoner in her own house. Grandma prevailed but Amelia's uncle was still not sure she would be welcomed at the meeting so he waited outside just in case.

"Once inside the auditorium Grandma sought to cover the child's head as best she could with her coat so that those who saw her wouldn't be frightened – for as she recalled, 'Her skin was now so badly cracked you could lay a pin in each crevice.'

"It was during the singing toward the end of the service, Amelia poked her grandmother. 'Look, Grandma,' she exclaimed in loud tones, 'I see Jesus up there.' 'Where?' her grandmother whispered. Heads turned all around them as the child said, 'Up there! At the side of Miss Kuhlman! Look at Him – Jesus up there! And see – He has His hands out!'

"Her grandmother looked down at Amelia and then she looked again, and her heart began to pound. The sores on the little girl's face were entirely dried up. There was no evidence of blood or pus anywhere to be seen. Her heart overflowed with joy and thanksgiving.

"When they left the building Amelia's uncle was waiting for them. He took one look at the little girl and nearly fainted. 'When we got home,' said her grandmother, 'She couldn't wait to tell everyone what had happened. The thing she told most was how she had seen Jesus. The thing her family saw was how her sores were all dried up. Her father took one look and cried, "A miracle!"' Within a week Amelia was completely free of any skin condition and totally healed. Her skin was flawless. Over one thousand people saw her condition and witnessed her healing which the doctors called a miracle.

"In the beginning, friends and neighbours, although they could not deny the healing, either accused the child of making up the story that she had seen Jesus or said the grandmother must have put it into the child's head. Even her mother and father were at first convinced that the whole thing had been a product of a child's over active imagination. They talked at length with her and questioned her closely, but nothing they could say could shake her insistence that she had seen Jesus with her own eyes."

When questioned by Miss Kuhlman Amelia reaffirmed that she had really seen Jesus the day she was miraculously healed. She said that Jesus stood next to Kathryn for at least five or ten minutes long after the singing had stopped. She said, “Miss Kuhlman I am positive it is the realist thing in my whole life.” Kathryn Kuhlman added, “I absolutely believe her.”

Why did little Amelia see Jesus and thousands of others including Miss Kuhlman didn’t? On the Damascus road Jesus appeared to Paul but the others there didn’t see Jesus yet knew something dramatic was taking place. Children often have great insight into the spiritual realm. When I was travelling and ministering in Brazil some years ago I visited one church in Uberlandia where I met people who had amazing encounters with God during a powerful visitation at their church. They said that as they worshipped the presence of God was so powerful and flecks of fine gold dust were floating in the air and covered their hands and faces. One young lad had a small nugget of gold in his thick, curly hair. These were mainly poor people who when they had the substance tested were told it was the purest gold. They added, “As we worshipped Jesus the children would often cry out they could see angels moving and ministering among us.”

Barry Dyck

It was 1974 and Barry Dyck was just eighteen-years-old studying in Bible College in British Columbia when he says he physically saw Jesus. He had badly injured himself while skiing at Mt Baker in Washington State nearby. Three vertebrae were broken in his back and he suffered a herniated disk. In excruciating pain he was rushed to St Mary’s Hospital in Bellingham, where he was placed in a neck brace and traction and kept as immobile as possible.

The following week was filled with fear and uncertainty as his ability to see became impaired by swelling in his head creating pressure on his brain. Surgery was scheduled to try and relieve the pressure.

During the middle of the night eights days after his accident something tremendous happened. Barry woke up and says he saw Jesus standing at the end of his bed with His arms stretched out towards him. Barry immediately sat up despite all the equipment attached to him and grasped the hands of Jesus and asked Him to "take me with you." Barry says he made this request because he was overwhelmed by an indescribable feeling of love. Jesus simply indicated that everything would be fine and Barry went back to a restless sleep. During the night he took off his neck brace that was limiting his movement. When he woke up the next morning he could see perfectly and the swelling in his head and all the pain had gone.

Barry says he was completely healed by Jesus during this encounter. He described Jesus as about six foot in height, and said His hair extended six inches below his shoulders. He does not know how he made the identification that this radiant figure was Jesus but it came to him immediately and without any question or doubt.

He managed to convince the doctors that he was well enough to go home. They had expected him to be in hospital for three months and in a neck brace for an additional eight months but within three days of returning home he was running and training without any ill effects.

While the numerous X-rays taken in the hospital after the accident clearly showed obvious signs of fracture, further X-rays taken by the family doctor in Seattle several weeks after Barry's encounter with Jesus showed no evidence whatsoever of any injury or fracture in his neck vertebrae having ever taken place. 2

John Occhipinti

John lives in Pennsylvania, USA, and is active as an evangelist and musician. He was brought up in a very devout Christian home in Connecticut, New Jersey, but did not become serious about his faith until he was about eighteen-years-old. The following year he went to Bible College in Texas and this was where, in 1958, his encounter with Jesus took place.

John was sharing a room with a fellow student called Nathan who, during November of that year, came down with a virus and stayed in bed to recover. John brought him food and prayed with him. As he was praying for him one night he opened his eyes to look at his friend lying about eight feet away and was shocked to see someone leaning over his bed, but facing and looking at him. John immediately identified the figure as that of Jesus because of the sense of awe that was invoked. John says that Jesus was as real to him as seeing an ordinary person and says he does not think that Nathan would have felt the touch on his head if it had been only a spiritual vision. Nathan later said that although he did not see anyone, he felt something touch his head.

Jesus appeared wearing a long white robe, shoulder length hair and a short beard. He seemed to be just under six foot tall and his skin was neither very dark nor very light, but His eyes seemed to be on fire.

He was just about to tell his sick friend what was happening when Jesus reached over and placed His hand on Nathan's forehead and disappeared. At that precise moment Nathan leaped out of his sick bed and ran down the halls of the dormitory shouting, "I've been healed, I've been healed." 3

13

JOHANNES FACIUS

God Can Do It Without Me

I have included this amazing account, even though Johannes never actually saw Jesus face to face, because he did have a very dramatic and personal encounter with Him. Jesus miraculously healed him, spoke to him and laid His physical hands upon him.

In 1985 Johannes took over the ministry of coordinating *Intercessors International* which quickly established in over 45 nations around the world. He was also the pastor of an independent church in Copenhagen and played a prominent role in the charismatic renewal in Scandinavia.

It was while leading a team of international intercessors and prayer leaders to Moscow in 1985, that he also experienced a powerful demonic attack. This was over the New Year of

1985/86, long before the breakdown of Communist control. Mikhail Gorbachev had been in office only a few months and the Soviet Union was still suffering under the dark cloud of Leninism.

The prayer team walked around the Kremlin, headquarters to the KGB and Russias secret police, praying for the downfall of the evil power which was still keeping so many Jews in bondage and preventing them from returning to Israel. They also walked to head office of the central committee of the Communist party where Gorbachev had his office. They went to let him know 'in spirit' that he was not the new ruler over the Soviet Union but that Jesus was. The prayer team also walked through the Lenin Mausoleum to pronounce God's judgment upon the god of the soviet system – an idol by the name of Vladimir Lenin, the founder of the Communist state. All over the Soviet Union at that time there were giant statues of Lenin and school children had to go to one of these each year and pay their respects to Lenin, to worship the father of the nation.

Before they went to the Lenin Mausoleum they sought God in prayer to know exactly what He wanted them to do. They knew they would not be allowed to stop and pray inside and they would have to keep walking following the long line of people filing past Lenin's tomb watched over by the many guards. Johannes received a word from God, Matthew 21:19, where Jesus spoke to the barren fig tree, *"May you never bear fruit again,"* and the tree then withered and died. The team understood from this they were to declare this proclamation in a whisper as they walked through the Mausoleum, "You spirit of death, we curse you in the name of the Lord Jesus. No one shall ever again eat fruit from you."

It was a few years later that the mighty demonic stronghold that gripped the Soviet Union was shattered but it was only a few hours later that Johannes experienced a strange spiritual attack that God allowed to fulfil His purposes. When

Johannes awoke the next morning he was so weak he could not get out of bed. After prayer from the team he was soon back on his feet but that was not to be the end for it was the start of three years of illness and depression.

Through this time Johannes knew that God was also at work and in his deepest pain and darkest moments God was there. He did not let the devil rob him in the darkness of what God had given to him in the light, but it was a long, dark valley.

Unable to continue in ministry he went to stay with good friends, a doctor and his wife, who offered to look after him and help nurse him back to health. A couple of weeks after being with them he says he experienced the most terrible day of his life and then the most amazing healing and encounter with Jesus.

It was February 24, 1989. At that time Johannes was still holding several ministry positions and spiritual leadership responsibilities. It was, he says, only a matter of time because of the pressures of ministry and responsibility that some kind of burn out or break down would hit him. The full force of that came upon him overwhelmingly on that February day. He decided that there was no way he could carry on with ministry and would have to give everything up.

He says, "A mixture of release and deep disappointment filled me as I lay down in my bed to sleep into what I believed would be a new secular life. I had no hope whatsoever for a turn around at this late hour. I did not believe God was interested in anything but dismissing me from the ranks of His servants. I felt disqualified, like a horse taken out of the race and put to grass, just waiting to die."

The next morning he woke up just before 5am with the sense that something unusual was happening within him, "I sat up in my bed looking around to see if there was someone in my room. Then I had this strange feeling that the early morning hours were quite different from those during the last three years. The real nightmare of my life would be the early hours of the morning, when the accusations and condemnation would come upon me with tremendous force, making me wish that I had never woken up. It is a well known fact among depressed people that the morning is the horror of their existence.

“But this morning things were different, and before I could even register what was so different and why, I felt as if a hand was laid upon my head and I became very hot. We old-time Pentecostals used to speak about a hot stream going through our bodies whenever we experienced some healing. This is what I felt. It was as if my two big toes had been put into the light socket on the wall. I became extremely hot all over for about thirty seconds, and after that three years of endless depression, accusation and condemnation vanished away like dew before the first rays of the rising sun.

“As an almost automatic reflex action I moved my hand over my chest to discover that my heart rhythm was back to normal. It was then I knew someone was in my room, although I could see no one with my physical eyes, and that someone was the Lord Jesus. One thirty second laying on of His wonderful hand had ended three years of suffering and torture. I knew it was the Lord because He spoke very clearly to me for the next ten minutes, and the light that flooded my soul was so bright that it not only covered all in the past, but gave me enough spiritual light for the rest of my life. All the scripture verses and portions that I had received over these last three years came alive and made eternal sense to me, just as if a button had been pushed on some hidden computer file and the whole programme lit up on the screen.

"Step by step the Lord explained all that I had been going through, not so much by examining 'why' as 'what for'. I am beginning to understand that our God is a God of divine purpose and destiny. He does not very often explain why, but He rather outlines for what purpose things have happened in our lives, and how He in His grace and mercy is making all things work for good.

"The first thing the Lord said was this, 'Johannes, all along this way you have been walking I have been longing to extend to you my healing touch, but I could not do it until you had been utterly broken before me. For in the days to come I cannot use you the way I have planned and give you my anointing in an increasing measure unless I know that your spirit is broken and your heart is contrite. I will not entrust my power and heavy anointing of my Spirit to anyone who has not been broken. I did this to you, Johannes, in order for you to know, and all others to know, that if in the future you are used with power and blessing in your ministry, everybody will know that it was I, and only I, who worked through you.'

"To me it was nothing less than being raised from the dead, a resurrection following the death of my own power and strength. It was a miracle, and its dramatic outworking is certainly the most powerful spiritual experience I have ever had. So remarkable was the change that it was hard for people to really believe what had happened, and it took almost eight months before I absorbed the power of God and come back to a more 'normal state'. The presence of Jesus was so powerful that I am deeply convinced I could not have stayed alive much longer in that consuming light and fire.

"As I realized I had been delivered, and after the Lord had left me, I jumped out of the bed and ran down the stairs into the kitchen, where Sven and Marianne were sitting at the breakfast table, because Marianne had to leave early for work. As I burst through the door with the joy and glory of the Lord on my face, Sven looked over his glasses with the puzzled gaze of a medical researcher as if he was trying to figure out whether I had gone completely mad. Then he said in a very convincing voice, 'Johannes, this cannot be the drugs, this must be the Lord!' and then all three of us began to laugh. This was the first laugh from me in three long and heavy years.

"Light, freedom, joy and peace flowed like a river through my soul. When all seemed finished and hopeless Jesus had raised me up from the grave and given me a totally new life. I never have been able, and never shall be able, to describe the feelings, the wonder of being whole, sane and sound.

"As long as I live and until I stand before God it will be my heart's delight to worship God and give honour and glory to His Son, the Lord Jesus, for pouring out upon my life streams of His grace in an abundance which turned my hopeless life completely around and gave me a new life full of future and hope."

14

DARRELL and ALISON PELL

"We Both Saw Jesus"

Cardiologist Dr Michael Sabom of St Joseph's Hospital in Atlanta, Georgia, USA, detailed the amazing account of Darrell Pell, a 34-year-old grocery store manager, who "died" (and then returned to life) while waiting for a heart transplant. What is significant about this vision and encounter is that not only did Darrell claim to see Jesus but so did his wife who was at his bedside.

The account is related in Dr Sabom's book, *Light and Death: One Doctor's Fascinating Account of Near -Death Experiences.* It took place at St Joseph's Hospital where Sabom worked on July 31, 1994. It was about 10am when an alarm went off indicating the first of what turned out to be a week of ten cardiac arrests for Darrell, multiple serious medical procedures, and a near decision to discontinue treatment to let him die.

Darrell admits he was not a practicing Christian at the time and had been struggling with drugs and alcohol but today he is a committed follower of Jesus Christ. Before this experience he said he never mentioned religion but now it's all he talks about. Following his experience the nurses would hear him singing the hymn *How Great Thou Art* – and once he recovered, he took to visiting bars and motorcycle meetings, attempting to convert those he encountered. His own motorcycle leather vest bore patches that said things like "Riding for the Son", "Christian Motorcycles Association", and "100 percent for Jesus".

The Encounter

During his first cardiac arrest Darrell says, "Suddenly, everything around me became an incredible sky blue, and I saw the faces of relatives and friends. Spontaneously, I began to recite the Scripture verse from Psalm 23 (about the *'valley of the shadow of death'*)."

As he did so he says he found his spirit hovering at ceiling level, watching as doctors and nurses scrambled to revive him. But Darrell wasn't watching alone. At his right side, he said, stood the Lord Jesus Christ, "with his left arm wrapped around me." He described Jesus as having reddish-brown hair that hung shoulder length.

There were four more cardiac arrests that day, recounts Dr Sabom, and only during the third did Darrell say Jesus spoke. Darrell says he asked the Lord what He wanted him to do and Jesus responded, "Go" – causing Darrell to return again into his body.

It had been a frantic day and around 11pm, friends, who had accompanied his wife Alison, had to go home, leaving her alone in her vigil. Although she too had stopped going to church years before, she

prayed, beseeching the Lord to save Darrell's life, and silently confessing her sins. "That's when I started asking for healing for Darrell," she recounted. "And that's when I opened my eyes and saw a light surrounding my husband's head, shoulders, and especially his heart. There was a gorgeous melding of white with gold that flowed like waves inside a 'lava lamp.' One beam hovered like a pillar over his chest," she told the cardiologist.

"I said, 'Lord, I'm going to open my eyes again, put your hand on his heart, and put your other hand on our hands and show me that this is real!' And when I opened my eyes, there was this person on Darrell's left side."

She saw Jesus' right hand on Darrell's heart and His left hand clasping her and her husband's hands.

She described Jesus as wearing a white robe with a blue sash, and had long brown hair. He was made of light, she said – yet somehow was not transparent.

"I closed my eyes and started giving thanks again," said Alison. "Darrell woke up a little later and I said, 'Did you know that Jesus was here?' He said, 'Yeah.' And I said, 'Where was He?' And he patted the bed right there where I saw Jesus!"

Deliverance and Direction Encounters

15

RICHARD WURMBRAND

Tortured For Christ

Pastor Richard Wurmbrand was an evangelical minister who was imprisoned and tortured for 14 years in Communist Romania. He was one of that country's most widely known Jewish Christian leaders, authors, and educators. In 1945, when the Communists seized Romania and attempted to control the churches, Wurmbrand immediately began an effective "underground" ministry to his enslaved people and the invading Russian soldiers.

On Sunday morning February 29, 1948, Pastor Wurmbrand set out on foot for church. He never arrived. For eight and a half years his wife Sabina and son did not know where he was or even whether he was alive or dead. "Ex-prisoners" assured her they had witnessed her husband's funeral in a Communist prison. She was heartbroken and yet she had her doubts. The men might be government stooges.

Wurmbrand's disappearance was expected. Anyone who acted contrary to the regime could expect imprisonment or death. At a "Congress of Cults" held by the Communist government, religious leaders promised to swear loyalty to the new regime. Sabrina asked Richard to "wipe the shame from the face of Jesus." He replied that if he stepped forward, she would no longer have a husband. "I don't need a coward for a husband," she answered. And so Wurmbrand stepped forward and told the 4,000 delegates that their duty as Christians was to glorify God and Christ alone.

He returned home to pastor an underground church and promote the gospel among Romania's Russian invaders. He smuggled Bibles into Russia, disguised as Communist propaganda. And then he disappeared.

As Wurmbrand walked to church that morning, a van full of secret police stopped in front of him. Four men jumped out and hustled him inside. He was taken to their headquarters and later locked in a solitary cell where he was designated "Prisoner Number 1."

His years of imprisonment consisted of a ceaseless round of torture and brainwashing. Sabrina herself was tortured for three years in prison.

Eight and a half years later, in 1956, Wurmbrand was released. He immediately recommenced secret church work and was returned to prison, not released again until 1964.

In 1965, realizing the great danger of a third imprisonment, Christians in Norway negotiated with the Communist authorities for his release from Romania. The "going price" for a prisoner was $1,900. Their price for Wurmbrand was $10,000.

He and his wife immediately spoke out for those still suffering in Communist hands. When he was asked to testify before the US Senate he showed them the eighteen holes cut in his body by his torturers.

Below is a part of the transcript of the evidence he gave that day on Friday, May 6, 1966, before a sub committee of the Congress of the United States Senate on the Communist Exploitation of Religion:

Senator Dodd

Were you in prison from 1948 to 1956?

Reverend Wurmbrand

Yes, and then imprisoned again in January 1959 to 1964.

Senator Dodd

Could you describe for us the cell in which you were kept in solitary confinement?

Reverend Wurmbrand

There were different cells in solitary confinement. I was in the first two nearly three years.

It was in the most beautiful building of Bucharest in the building of the Secretariat of State for Internal Affairs. It is a building before which all foreigners stand and admire. I can tell you that your White House is a very little building in comparison with ours. And there ten metres beneath the earth are the cells. There are no windows in the cells. Air enters through a tube. And there were a few desks with a mattress – a straw mattress. You had only three steps for a walk. Never were we taken out from these cells except for interrogations when prisoners were beaten and tortured.

For years I never saw the sun, moon, flowers, snow, stars – no man except the interrogator who beat me, but I can say I have seen heaven open, I have seen Jesus Christ, I have seen the angels and we were very happy there.

But the treatment was very bad. The purpose was to make us mad. You didn't hear a noise. A whisper you didn't hear in this cell. The guards had felt shoes. In all those years of prison we never had a book, we never had a piece of paper, we never had a newspaper, nothing to distract our mind except that from time to time tape recorders were put on in the corridor. I didn't know what a tape recorder was. I had not seen such a thing. But at once we heard beautiful Romanian music, and then we enjoyed it. We didn't know what had happened with the Communists that they made us enjoy such music but after 10 or 15 minutes you heard screams, “Ha, ha, ha don't beat,” the torturing of a woman. This lasted for half an hour, and of 100 prisoners who had been in that cell, in that corridor, everybody recognized that it is his wife or that it is his girl. I myself thought also that it was my wife.

One Sunday morning, in the prison at Pitesti, a young Christian was already the fourth day, day and night, tied to a cross. Twice a day the cross was put on the floor and 100 other cell inmates by beating and torture, were forced to fulfill their necessities upon his face and upon his body. Then the cross was erected again and the Communists swearing and mocking said, “Look your Christ, look your Christ, how beautiful he is, adore him, kneel before him, how fine he smells, your Christ.”

Senator Dodd

How did the Romanian secret police employ brainwashing techniques?

Reverend Wurmbrand

The worst thing was the brainwashing. All the tortures of times before were nothing in comparison with brainwashing.

First of all we were drugged. The drugs were put in our food. I did not know about this dope. But we saw the results. First of all there was lack of power of will. It was completely broken. If we were told, "Lift your hand," I lifted it. If I was not told to let the hand down, I would never have let it down.

We were at the same time very much undernourished. We had times when we received 100 grams, one slice of bread, a week. It was told to us, "We give you only as many calories as you need to be able to breathe," and so our power of will was broken.

Second, this drug or perhaps it is another drug, produces the delirium of self accusation. I have seen prisoners knocking on the door during the night and saying, "Take me to the interrogator, I have new things to say against myself." Prisoners quarreled with their interrogators to say against themselves more than the interrogators asked from them. And then we have had in prisons the curious phenomenon that we as priests received confessions from other prisoners. Now everybody is a sinner, but not everybody is a criminal. Men who have never murdered confessed that they have murdered, that they have committed adultery and that they have stolen. They felt they had to accuse themselves.

That is the secret of all the Soviet show trials, in which the prisoners accuse themselves. For seventeen hours a day from five in the morning to ten in the evening we had to sit still. We were not allowed to lean. We were not allowed to rest even a little bit our weary heads upon our hands. To close your eyes was a crime. Seventeen hours a day we had to sit like that and hear from the morning to the evening, "Communism is good! Communism is good! Communism is good!, Communism is good!" until you heard one who was 20 years in prison under the Communists shouting, "Communism is good! Communism is good! Communism is good! I give my life for Communism!"

In prison there were not only priests and pastors. We had hundreds of peasants and young boys and girls who were put in prison for their Christian faith. These were separated and for them there was a special brainwashing, not only that "Communism is good!" but "Christianity is dead! Christianity is dead! Christianity is dead! Nobody believes in Christ any more, nobody believes in Christ, you are the only fools!"

They gave us post cards. I had not seen my wife for ten years. They gave me post cards, they gave to all of us post cards: "Write to your children and wife; they may come and on that day see you and bring you parcels," so on that day we were shaved; we expected and expected until the evening and nobody came. They had not sent the post cards, but we did not know. Then came more brain washings. "Your wives are laying in bed with men." Obscene words, "Your children hate you. You have nobody to love in the world. You are only fools! Give up faith. Nobody is Christian any more! Christianity is dead!"

I believed also that there were no longer any Christians. I had read in the Bible that there will be in the last time the great apostasy, that people will leave the faith and I believed that I lived now at this time. But I said to myself if Christianity is dead, I will sit at its tomb and will weep until it arises again, just as Mary Magdalene sat at the tomb of Jesus and wept until Jesus showed Himself. Then when I came out of prison I saw Christianity is not dead. The number of practicing Christians in Romania according to the figures given by the Communists themselves in twenty years of Communist dictatorship had grown three hundred per cent.

Senator Dodd

I have many more questions, but would you show your wounds and scars, if you have some?

Reverend Wurmbrand

I apologize here before the ladies.

Senator Dodd

Take your time. If ever a man was entitled to time, I think you are.

Reverend Wurmbrand

Look here, look here, look here. Look here, look here. And so the whole body.

Senator Dodd

What is the scar behind your ear?

Reverend Wurmbrand

Here they put the knife and said, "Give accusatory statement against your bishops and against the other pastors. Do you give or not?" And they cut. It is true that they did not cut very deeply.

Senator Dodd.

These are all knife wounds?

Reverend Wurmbrand

They tortured by all means. They beat until they broke the bones. They used red-hot irons, they used knives, they used everything. And what was the main thing is not that they beat, not what they did, but how they did it. They interrogated you very politely, and if you did not wish to say what they asked they said, “Well, today is the 1st. on the 15th you will be beaten and tortured at 10 o'clock in the evening.”

Imagine what the next 14 days were like after this. We had prisoners who during this time, knocked at the cell door, “I can't bear it. I will say everything,” before their time for torture came.

Senator Dodd

I wish you would turn around before you put your shirt on.

Reverend Wurmbrand

And that it may be very clear, it is not that I boast with these marks. I show to you the tortured body of my country, of my fatherland, and of my church, and they appeal to the American Christians and to all freemen of America to think about our tortured body, and we do not ask you to help us. We ask you only one thing. Do not help our oppressors and do not praise them. You cannot be a Christian and praise the inquisitors of Christians. That is what I have to say.

Senator Dodd

All right. You may put on your clothes. That scar on your right breast, do you remember how that was inflicted?

Reverend Wurmbrand

Yes, by knife.

I have been in Oslo. I went to a hospital. There were several physicians. I can give their names. I spoke with them about religion. In the beginning they said, “We are atheists,” and then they saw my body and I asked them what treatment do I need. They said, “About treatment, do not ask us. Ask only the one in whom we don't believe, but who has kept you alive, because according to our medical books, you are dead. A man who has what you have, with four vertebras broken, cannot live. According to our medical books, you are dead. If you are alive, then the one in whom we don't believe has kept you alive."

I must tell you I was in England before I came to the States, and I have spoken with high Christian officials from England. The Archbishop of Canterbury and many canons and so on have been in our country recently, last year. So I asked these Christian leaders – I will not tell names – "Why have you sat at banquets with our inquisitors? I am a little pastor, I cannot interrogate you, but I speak for the others who cannot speak for themselves. Why have you sat at banquets with our inquisitors?"

I was answered, "We are Christians and must have friendship and fellowship with everybody, with the Communists, too. Don't you agree?"

I said, "I can't polemicize with you. I have not read the Bible for 14 years. You must know Christianity better than I. Faintly I remember in the Bible it is written that friendship with the world is hatred toward God. But supposing you must have friendship and fellowship with everybody. How is it that you have had friendship and fellowship only with our inquisitors and never with us?"

Never have these great men of the West been in the houses of Christian martyrs. I have an only son and I love him. I cannot look to him. He looks like a skeleton. He has hungered. He will never be healthy. And so many of our children died. All these great prelates from the West are great men. I am very little in comparison with them. But I always asked myself, "Well, all right, have friendship with the Communists. But why only with the Communists?" They never inquired about us.

Richard Wurmbrand's testimony was carried across newspapers in the US, Europe, and Asia. Afterward, he was invited to speak before hundreds of groups. By 1967, "Prisoner Number 1" had established the mission organization that is now known as *Voice of the Martyrs,* dedicated to assisting those who suffer for Christ throughout the world.

Richard and Sabina were able to survive their ordeal through the power of love. "If the heart is cleansed by the love of Jesus Christ," wrote Wurmbrand, "and if the heart loves Him, you can resist all tortures."

While in prison he had many supernatural experiences with Jesus. He testified of this in the Senate hearing. He heard Jesus' audible voice and describes an amazing encounter he had on another occasion,

"At once the walls of the cell began to shine like diamonds. I have heard Bach, I have heard Beethoven in my life, I have seen California and I have seen Napoli, I have seen many beautiful things but never have I seen the beauties I have seen in the dark cell beneath the earth.

"Never have I heard such beautiful music as on that day the King of Kings – Jesus – was with us.

"We saw His understanding, His lovely eyes. He wiped away from our eyes our tears. He said to us words of love and words of forgiveness, we knew that everything which had been evil in our lives had past away and had been forgotten by God.

"Now there came wonderful days. The bride was in the arms of the Bridegroom. We were with Christ, we didn't know we were in prison."

16

SAMUEL DOCTORIAN

And Then I saw Him

Samuel Doctorian is an Armenian born in 1930 in the city of Beirut. When he was just nine-years-old he committed his life to Christ as he stood at the place in Jerusalem where Jesus was crucified, he there resolved that his whole life would be lived for Him.

Coming from a poor family, at the age of fourteen, he could not continue his schooling, and started work in a shoe maker's shop. It was there that he describes how he first clearly heard the audible voice of Jesus calling him to the ministry.

"I was busy sewing shoes. I heard clearly the voice of the Lord. It was not a kind of impression or imagination. I heard with my ears my name being

called. The Lord said these following words, in my own language: 'Samuel, Samuel, leave everything and follow me. I will make you a fisher of men.' Of course I trembled. I was scared. I fell on my knees. I dropped the shoes on the floor. I bowed before that voice, and began to cry. I remember saying, 'Lord, what can I do? I come from such a poverty stricken home. I've had so many struggles, difficulties, trials. I was unable to continue my education. I had to leave school just starting on the fifth grade. What can I do Lord?'

"I felt there was a mistake. Why should the Lord call me? How can it be? But I heard the voice of the Lord a second time saying, 'I will make you.' I quickly said, 'Lord, if you will make me, I believe you. What little I have one hundred percent is yours; my mind, my talents, my strength, my youth, my future all belongs to you. I leave everything on the altar of the Lord.'"

By miraculous answers to prayer God opened a Bible School in Jerusalem in which Samuel enrolled. One day there while fasting and praying the Lord sent an angel to him. Samuel says,

"I had never seen an angel before and never heard their voices. This was the first time in my life at the age of 16, just turning 17. An angel of the Lord came. I saw him. He said to me, 'Come with me, Samuel.' With tremendous joy, I went with him. I didn't know how it happened, since I was on my knees, and at the same time, I knew I was with the angel. I went with him in my spirit. As I walked with the angel of the Lord, he brought me into a heavenly glorious place, where I witnessed a multitude of people. As I was standing in the back, I could see the throne of God.

"On the throne was my precious Saviour, the Lord Jesus. He called me by my name. Everybody turned around to see who is this Samuel. I was so small, I felt just like a little lad. As I was walking down the aisle, everybody was looking at me. I went with fear and trembling and fell before the Lord. The Lord said, 'I have heard your prayers. I will answer you. I will take you to America.' Immediately I said, 'When, when Lord?' He said, 'Wait and you will see.' I said, 'But Lord, I don't have any money or ways and means to go.' The Lord answered me, 'All riches belong to me. I will give you whatever you need.'

"I praised Him and glorified His name. Then the angel of the Lord told me to come back with him, which I did. He brought me back to my room where I was on my knees praying. You can imagine my tremendous joy and surprise. For a long time I could not get up from my knees. I was praising God and glorifying His wonderful name. From that day on I never asked the Lord again when I would go to America. He had told me to 'wait and see.' In 1955 at the age of 25 this miraculously came to pass. Since then I have been to the United States of America 162 times."

God has used Samuel in many countries all over the Middle East, Europe, North and South America and other parts of the world to bring revival. He has ministered in over 120 nations. Besides his amazing encounter with Jesus he has seen angels on more than ten occasions. Each time it has been a powerful and real experience not just sensing their presence but actually seeing them and hearing their audible voice.

He tells of the time he was ministering in Asyut in Upper Egypt and saw one of the greatest and mightiest moves of the Holy Spirit he had ever witnessed. One of those saved in the revival meetings was a colonel who had a high position in the Egyptian government. He had recently moved to become the governor of the second largest prison in Egypt which was in Asyut. He attended the revival meetings every night and brought some of the prisoners with their guards to the services. Samuel continues,

"One day the colonel invited me to go to his home for a few hours of relaxation. He asked me if I wanted to see the gallows where they hang the criminals and murderers. I had never seen one before and although it was not the best sight to see I was very interested. 'Yes,' I said. It was a terrible room. What an awful sight. I asked the colonel if there were any that were 'soon to be hung?' 'Yes,' he said, 'there are three men and two women. I'm waiting for their orders from the court in Cairo.' I said, 'Do you also hang women?' He said, 'Of course, although we haven't done it for a long time.' I asked, 'What have these criminals done?' I heard dreadful stories. 'Can I see the women in their cells?' I asked. He took me to the women's section of the prison.

"I came to one of the doors. They opened a little window, and I looked inside. I saw the first woman. They said she was 54-years-old. She looked like a witch. She looked horrible. She had killed her former husband with an axe, while he was sleeping in the field, just because he had married another woman.

"I looked into the other cell. A young women of 23 was in there. The moment she saw me looking through that little window she started crying and shouting, 'Help me! Help me!' Suddenly I couldn't look any more. I was going to cry. I asked the colonel, 'What has she done?' 'Well it's an awful story,' he said. 'She killed a 12-year-old girl and stole her earrings. She had tried to sell them to buy opium, hashish, for her husband.' 'Then she's married,' I remarked. 'Oh yes,' the colonel answered, 'and she has three children.' It was a heart breaking story. I couldn't bear hearing any more.

"When I went back again to the colonel's home I couldn't think of anything else. All I could see in front of me was the face of that young 23-year-old mother crying, 'Help me, help me.' What could I do?

"The prison guards drove me back to the home where I was staying in the city of Asyut. I was ready to have my afternoon nap to get ready for the night meeting. I fell on my knees to pray, but I still saw that woman's face and I heard, 'Help me, help me.' I began to pray. 'Lord, is there something I could do?' That's all I said. Suddenly my room was filled with the presence of the Lord. With my eye, I could see an angel of the Lord in front of me. He did not speak but he had a scroll in his hand. He opened the scroll, and I could read very clearly the message from the Lord.

"'That young mother is not the murderer. She did not kill that girl. Her husband killed the girl. But he threatened his wife, and told her that she should confess to the murder. He said that the government would not punish women as severe as men, so in a couple of years she would be out of prison. But if she wouldn't confess, then her husband threatened to kill her and her three children. The young mother with fear and trembling lied. She confessed she was the murderer.'

"When I got that message I was shaken to the depth of my soul. I went straight to the telephone, called the colonel, and said, 'Come quickly, I must talk with you.' He said, 'What is it?' I said, 'I cannot talk over the telephone. This is something extremely important.' Although he is a commander and has tremendous authority, he is my spiritual son. He loves and respects me very much. He said, 'I will come immediately.' He came with his guards and soldiers. He came right up to the room where I was. I said, 'Colonel, sit down on that chair. Let me tell you what happened.' I told him how the angel of the

Lord came, where he stood and the message he gave me. The colonel was shocked, shaken and bewildered. He said, 'You really mean an angel? A heavenly angel came right there?' I said, 'Yes, right there and more importantly this is the message the angel gave me.' The colonel said, 'I don't know what to do. It's not in my hand. The court case is closed. Confessions have been heard. Any instant the orders come from the court in Cairo, I must hang the woman.' I said, 'You dare not do it. She's not the murderer. The angel told me so.'

"'What do you want me to do?' he asked. I said, 'Go back to the prison now. That dear woman is going to confess to you the exact truth. And when that woman tells you word by word what the angel told me, what better confirmation do you want?' He said, 'I've never heard anything like this in all my life. I'm going immediately.'

"As the colonel arrived at the prison and entered the gates one of his officers informed him that one of the women awaiting execution wanted to speak with him. He asked, 'Who?' They said, 'The younger one.' He ordered, 'Bring her in.' He secretly got a tape recorder ready in his office. When she entered the young woman was trembling, afraid, a little bit ashamed, with just a sack over her body. As she walked in, she asked if she could speak to the colonel alone. He agreed. They all left the room and the tape recorder was switched on. That young, dear mother confessed with tears, word by word, exactly what the angel of the Lord had told me. The tapes went to Cairo. The judges heard the whole story. The real murderer was caught, judged and found guilty. The young mother, with her three children, was taken to a totally different village. They were placed there secretly so the relatives of the husband would not know where they were. And thank God they're alive to this day.

"The whole story was told in all of the official newspapers in Egypt."

17

GUL MASIH and OSWALDO MAGDANGAL

In the Midst of the Furnace

It's not hard to make bold statements of faith when everything is going well but the real testing of our trust in God is when living for Him brings us more tribulation than we ever imagined. One of my best friends is in hospital as I type this and he has just heard that he has inoperable cancer with three to twelve months to live. He wrote on his internet website, "I do not want to die and leave my family and I am believing for Jesus to heal me. My trust is in Him. The Lord gives and the Lord takes away, blessed be the name of the Lord."

There are many different levels of faith. Jesus spoke about little faith and those with great faith. Three men in the Old Testament, Shadrach, Meshach and Abednego, come into the latter category – because they wouldn't bow down to worship the emperor's golden image they were to be executed. They were thrown into a furnace so hot and fierce that the guards who opened the doors were themselves consumed. We read the story in Daniel chapter three.

> *"If we are thrown into the blazing furnace, the God we serve is able to save us from it, and he will rescue us from your hand, O king. But even if he does not, we want you to know, O king, that we will not serve your gods or worship the image of gold you have set up."*

When they were thrown into the fire something amazing happened, not only did they remain unharmed but a fourth person appeared with them and Nebuchadnezzar was "gob smacked," that's the ultra-modern translation which captures the original really well.

> *"Then King Nebuchadnezzar leaped to his feet in amazement and asked his advisers, "Weren't there three men that we tied up and threw into the fire?" They replied, "Certainly, O king." He said, "Look! I see four men walking around in the fire, unbound and unharmed, and the fourth looks like a son of the gods."*

Jesus was there with them and not only were they unharmed but the only part of them affected by the flames was the ropes that bound them that had burned away. It was a day they would never forget nor the King who consequently promoted them and acknowledged their God.

Gul Masih

Gul Masih was imprisoned and sentenced to death in Pakistan for his faith in Jesus Christ. He was condemned on a charge of blasphemy against the prophet Mohammed. His case was widely reported by the world's press and Amnesty International which highlighted the use and abuse of Pakistan's blasphemy laws against Christians.

Pakistan's penal code allows for the death penalty for directly or indirectly defiling “the sacred name of the holy Prophet Mohammed.” It also stipulates a ten year prison sentence for insulting the religion of any class of citizens, and provides for a sentence of life imprisonment for “whoever willfully defiles, damages, or desecrates a copy of the holy Koran.”

Masih was the first person to be sentenced to death for blasphemy since the death penalty became mandatory in 1991. He was a resident of eastern Sargodha, a town about 200 miles from Islamabad which has a sizable Christian minority.

On December 10, 1991, Masih and his long time neighbour Mohammad Sajjad Hussain, a Muslim, were engaged in conversation at their community water tap. According to Masih, the tap was broken, and he had commented that the plumber who had collected the community money to fix it was dishonest. The plumber was a Muslim. Eyewitnesses and participants have offered conflicting accounts of the rest of the conversation.

Hussain claimed that Masih cursed the plumber and made derogatory comments about the neighbourhood, Pakistan and Islam. He also claimed that Masih made derogatory remarks about the Prophet Mohammed, and that an argument then developed between the two men.

Other reports of the day's events did not mention any such confrontation. No other witnesses supported Sajjad Hussain's claim. Two eye-witnesses, Muhammad Safdar and Ghulam Hussain, have denied that Masih committed blasphemy. Father Philip, of the Sargodha parish, stated that the conversation at the water tap did turn from politics to religion, but he described it as a conversational exchange rather than a fight. Gul Masih's brother Bashir stated that the two men parted after shaking hands and hugging each other.

Under Section 295-C of the penal code both Gul Masih and his brother Bashir were charged with blasphemy. Sajjad was supposed to have made a comment stating that the Virgin Mary must have been a prostitute. Masih, in turn, replied he had read "that Mohammed had 11 wives, including a minor."

On December 14, 1991, Gul and Bashir were detained by the police overnight and then transferred to jail. After a number of Muslim neighbours testified that Bashir had not participated in the conversation, he was released after spending a month and a half in jail. Yet several local clerics demanded that he be rearrested and that both men be hanged. Statements to this effect were made at Friday prayers and appeared on posters.

Gul Masih's trial commenced in November 1992. Sajjad Hussain was the only witness to testify that Gul had said anything blasphemous. Although Hussain claimed that two eye-witnesses also heard the blasphemous remarks, both testified that Gul Masih was innocent of the charge. Nevertheless, on the basis of Sajjad Hussain's testimony alone, the Additional Sessions Judge of Sargodha, Khan Talib Hussain Baloch, sentenced Gul Masih to death by hanging, and a fine of Rs. 5,000 [$200], subject to confirmation by the High Court.

Gul was held in solitary confinement. According to his brother, Aziz, Gul was beaten up by another prisoner reportedly as punishment for the crime of blasphemy. When he met with representatives of the Human Rights Commission, Masih was brought in handcuffs and appeared to have been physically mistreated.

Gul Masih was sentenced to death by the Sessions Court and had to languish in jail until the Division Bench of the Lahore High Court, in its judgement of October 27, 1994, declared that this was a "Case of no evidence." Subsequently, he was acquitted and released from jail.

It was difficult however, to release him from jail as a serious threat had been made against his life by Muslim extremists who were angry over his acquittal. Consequently, he was taken out of the prison at night under the protection of a heavy police contingent to a safe place from where he was transferred to Islamabad airport and flown to Germany under an arrangement with church officials.

While in prison he wrote a long letter to those who prayed for him. Part of it read as follows,

> **"My dear friends, my Lord has come to me twice in my prison cell. One day I was sitting in my prison thinking about this injustice in a sad and hopeless mood. Suddenly, my cell was filled with light and my body trembled. I saw my Lord.**
>
> **"Four days later my Jesus came again and overshadowed me by raising His hands and blessing me. From that day on I have been happy and in peace. My Lord is with me in jail. He does not leave me alone."**

Oswaldo Magdangal

Though his birth name is Oswaldo Magdangal, he is fondly known as Pastor Wally by friends and family. Magdangal is a Filipino who worked in Riyadh and became the founding pastor of an active secret Christian fellowship and director of a secret Bible school in Saudi Arabia, where 300 to 700 people gathered to worship and whose graduates helped pioneer churches in many countries.

The church and Bible school had to meet in secret because there has not been an official church of any kind in Saudi Arabia for almost fourteen hundred years. Those who gathered to worship Jesus knew the risk they were taking.

Magdangal said, “Every time we came together, we made people aware that this may be their first or even last time to be in a church in that place, at anytime the police can come in and take us all to prison.”

Islam was founded in Saudi Arabia more than 1300 years ago. For Muslims the Arabian peninsula became the centre of the world. The two holiest mosques of Islam are located in Saudi Arabia, and today more than one billion Muslims turn five times a day towards Mecca in prayer (or rather they should if they are faithful Muslims). It has also resulted in millions of Muslims coming to Saudi Arabia for the annual *hajj* pilgrimage.

Islam seeks to provide a framework for all thinking. The Koran does not provide answers for all questions of life and the problems encountered in daily life, but Muslims can always turn to the *Hadieth*, the example set by Mohammed in his lifetime which still determines the life of every faithful Muslim. The central theme in Islam is the “Oneness of Allah,” which is (or rather should be) reflected in the Oneness of Society (the *umma*).

What this means for the world view of Muslims is also clear. Muslims define the world in two separate realms: the *Dar el Islam* (the world where Islam rules), and the *Dar el Harb* (literally “the house of war”). This is the part of the world still to be conquered by Islam. Since Islam sees itself as the superior religion, all non-Muslims are seen as potential converts or enemies.

The Christian church in Saudi Arabia is living under the most difficult circumstances. Freedom of religion does not exist. The government prohibits the practice of other religions, be it in public or in private. Saudi law states that no churches may be built north of Yemen and south of Jordan. It is impossible for foreigners to visit Saudi Arabia as tourists. One can only enter the kingdom on a business visa (ie on the invitation of a company already active in the country), or as a Muslim pilgrim.

The Saudi religious police (*Mutawwa'in*) are practically omnipresent in Saudi Arabia. Their power is almost limitless. The *Mutawwa'in* have special prisons where they torture their victims. Their behaviour is often ruthless and their aim is to ascertain that all citizens (and expatriates) adhere to strict Islamic legislation.

The religious police see it as their main task to track down believers of other religions and to prevent their gatherings. For this reason they have constructed a wide network of informers. Meetings of Christians therefore have to take place in the deepest secrecy. These secret gatherings are hunted down with increasing diligence and the leaders subjected to humiliating beatings, imprisonment and expulsion from the country. This is particularly so for the Asian Christians who have been the most effective witnesses for Jesus. Few expatriates have meaningful contacts with Saudis under these circumstances.

This is also one of the reasons why expatriate Christians are reluctant to admit Saudi nationals to their meetings. Expatriate Christians live under strict surveillance. They can show no outward signs of being a Christian. They are only allowed to meet informally in people's homes or at embassy compounds. They must be very careful especially with Christmas holidays when the *Mutawwa'in* further step up their already all prevailing surveillance.

The *Mutawwa'in* control every aspect of daily life. They patrol the streets in their cars, check in shops if women are dressed according to Islamic dress codes, see that all shops are closed during prayer times, watch that no signs of other religions are visible etc.

Systematic discrimination based on sex and religion is built into Saudi law. By religious law and social custom women have the right to own property and are entitled to financial support from their husbands or male relatives. However, women have few political and social rights and are not treated as equal members of society. There are no active women's rights groups, nor would one be tolerated by the Government. Women, including foreigners, may not legally drive motor vehicles or ride bicycles and are restricted in their use of public facilities when men are present. Women must enter city buses by separate rear entrances and sit in specially designated sections. Women risk arrest by the *Mutawwa'in* for riding in a vehicle driven by a male who is not an employee or a close male relative. Women are not admitted to a hospital for medical treatment without the consent of a male relative. By law and custom, women may not undertake domestic and foreign travel alone.

The number of expatriate Christians in Saudi Arabia is high. The number of (nominal) Christians is several hundreds of thousands, but the number of practising Christians is only a fraction of that. When they suspect a person, the *Mutawwa'in* will not hesitate to bug telephones, perform house searches, or to follow people.

In fact, one can say that there are three "layers" of churches in Saudi Arabia: the "tolerated fellowships" on compounds and in embassies, the underground evangelical house groups meeting in private homes, and the secret believers who do not meet in larger groups.

The gatherings on compounds and in embassies are more or less formal, but they can only happen when Christians keep a low profile and allow no Saudis to join their meetings. Yet Christians in Saudi Arabia have stated that their underground, expatriate church is strong.

In late 1992, after ten years of ministry, Magdangal was arrested and shackled, thrown into a three by four foot cell, stripped, and subjected to sleep deprivation, brainwashing attempts, and flogging. Once he was tortured for three-and-a-half hours by three Muslim clerics who demanded he provide the names of other Christians.

"Eventually, I was so weak they placed the pad of paper in my lap, and they forced the pencil into my hand," Magdangal told *Christianity Today* (a leading Evangelical magazine). "I was weeping, and I said, 'Lord, you've got to help me here,' and I began to write the names of Billy Graham, Charles Spurgeon, and others. After a few days they were so mad because they'd been all over Saudi Arabia looking for those people."

Despite the brutal torture and cruel mistreatment he suffered from his captors, Magdangal did not feel any kind or any type of bitterness at all, nor hatred towards these people. He even prayed for them. "I said, 'Lord, these people do not understand what they're doing. Do not take this up against them.'"

Magdangal was sentenced to die on Christmas Day because it happened to fall that year on a Friday, the Muslim day of rest and the day executions typically occur. But Magdangal was spared death when an international outcry convinced Saudi King Fahd bin Abdul al-Aziz Al Saud to overrule the *Mutawwa'in* and order him released and deported on Christmas Eve. Magdangal arrived in Manila on Christmas Day, 1992.

"It was a miracle of God," Magdangal said.

He Saw Jesus

Immediately after his arrest Magdangal says he was slapped, boxed and kicked in the face. Then using a long stick, they lashed his back and the palms of his hands, then the soles of his feet. He could not stand without wincing and he describes his bruised body as looking like an eggplant.

Upon returning to his cell, he prayed for five hours thanking God for allowing him to participate in the sufferings of Jesus.

He describes what happened next,

> **"Suddenly, there was light. The cell was filled with the Lord's Shekinah glory. His presence was there. He knelt and started to touch my face. He told me, 'My son, I have seen all of it, that's why I'm here. I'm assuring you that I will never leave you or forsake you.'"**

Magdangal awoke two hours later feeling like a new man. He was amazed when he saw his body had been restored to perfect wholeness. No bruises, no cuts, no bleeding or blood stains. He said, "God had completely restored me."

After his release, he founded Christians in Crisis, a group that works to raise awareness about the 200 million believers in at least 60 nations worldwide who face persecution for their belief in Jesus. Today he travels the world sharing about God's love and mercy.

18

BROTHER YUN

The Heavenly Man

In 2002 a book was published about the remarkable story of a Chinese evangelist, known as Brother Yun, and called *The Heavenly Man*. His life, ministry, persecution and suffering are truly astonishing.

His miraculous escape from Zhengzhou Number One Maximum Security Prison in the Henan Province of China reads like a scene from the Acts of the Apostles.

After suffering excruciating torture with his legs smashed and body battered and bruised Yun amazingly managed to walk out of the prison to freedom. He recounts,

"Lying on the floor of my cell I had a powerful vision come to me even though I was wide awake. I saw my wife, Deling, sitting beside me. She had just been released from prison and was preparing some medicine. She lovingly treated my wounds. I felt greatly encouraged and asked her, 'Have you been released?' She replied, 'Why don't you open the iron door?' Before I could answer she walked out of the room and the vision ended.

"The Lord spoke to me, 'This is the hour of your salvation.' Immediately I knew that this was a vision from the Lord, and that I was meant to try and escape.

"I called to the guard. He came to my door and asked me what I wanted. I told him, 'I need to go to the toilet right now.' Because it was Brother Xu's job to carry me around, the guard opened his door and ordered him to carry me to the bathroom.

"Each floor of the prison was protected by an iron gate. Normally two guards were stationed on either side of every gate, so to make it to the prison courtyard I would have to go through three iron gates on three floors, and pass six guards. Brother Xu came to my door. As soon as he saw me he commanded me, 'You must escape!'

"It was now six weeks since my legs had been smashed. Even putting a little weight on them caused tremendous agony but I believed that the Lord had told me in three different ways that I was to try to escape – through His Word, through the vision of my wife, and through Brother Xu.

"It was just before eight o'clock on the morning of May 5, 1997. To the natural mind, this time of day was the worst possible time to try to escape! There was normally so much activity throughout the prison, with all the guards at their posts. I shuffled out of my cell and walked towards the locked iron gate in the hallway. I looked straight ahead and prayed beneath my breath with every step. At the exact moment I reached the gate, another servant of the Lord, Brother Musheng, was returning to his cell and the gate was opened for him. As he passed me I told him, 'Wait! Don't close the gate.' I walked through without even breaking my stride! The Lord's timing was perfect!

"There had been a guard accompanying Musheng back to his cell, but at the exact moment he opened the gate for Musheng, a telephone rang in an office down the hallway and the guard turned and ran to answer it.

"An armed guard was positioned at his desk facing the second iron gate. At that moment the Holy Spirit spoke to me, 'Go now! The God of Peter is your God!' Somehow the Lord seemed to blind that guard. He was staring directly at me, yet his eyes didn't acknowledge my presence at all. I expected him to say something, but he just looked through me as if I was invisible! He didn't say a word.

"I continued past him and didn't look back. I knew I could be shot in the back at any moment. I walked down the stairs, but nobody stopped me and none of the guards said a word to me!

"When I arrived at the main iron gate leading out to the courtyard I discovered it was already open! This was strange, as it was usually the most secure gate of all. There were normally two guards stationed at the first floor gate, one on the inside and one on the outside, but for some reason neither of the guards was present and the gate was open!

"The bright morning light made me wince. I walked past several guards in the yard but nobody said a word to me. I then strolled through the main gate of the prison, which for some strange reason was also standing ajar! My heart was pounding! I was now standing on the street outside the Zhengzhou Number One Maximum Security Prison! I was told later that nobody had ever escaped from that prison before."

Yun made it to safety and God miraculously made it possible for him and his family to leave China and they now live in Germany from where he travels around the world ministering.

Many years before, as a young man zealous for the Lord, he tells of a defining moment in his life when he had an amazing encounter with Jesus and heard His audible voice.

"I began to wait on the Lord for His guidance and a wonderful thing happened. One night around 10pm – before my parents had gone to bed – I had just

completed a time of prayer and had memorized Acts 12. As I lay down on my bed I suddenly felt someone tap my shoulder and heard a voice tell me, 'Yun, I am going to send you to the west and south to be my witness.'

"Thinking it was my mother speaking, I jumped out of my bed and went to my parents' room. I asked her, 'Did you call my name? Who tapped me on my shoulder?'

"My mother said, 'Neither of us called for you. Go back to sleep.' I prayed again and climbed into bed.

"Thirty minutes later again lying down I heard a clear voice that urged me, 'Yun, you shall go to the west and the south to proclaim the gospel. You shall be my witness and will testify on behalf of my name.'

"Immediately I got up and told my mother what had happened. She told me to go back to sleep and asked me not to be so excited. She was concerned I was losing my mind!

"I knelt down and prayed to the Lord, 'Jesus, if you're speaking to me, then I am listening. If you are calling me to preach your good news, then I'm willing to obey your call on my life.'

"Later that night I received a dream from the Lord confirming what I had been told. In the dream a young man came out of a crowd and asked, 'Are you Brother Yun? Our brothers and sisters have been fasting and praying for you for three days. We hope you will come to our midst and preach the gospel to us. We desperately need you to come to our village.'

"The next morning I told my mother that the previous night 'the Lord spoke to me three times and I will be obedient to the heavenly call.' That morning I left my home village and started walking toward the west. When I crossed a bridge I met an old Christian man whose name was Yang. He asked me where I was going. I replied, 'This morning the Lord spoke to me three times. He wants me to preach the gospel in the west and the south.' Brother Yang's heart was deeply moved. He said, 'Right now I was on my way to see you. I was given the job to come and take you to the west, to Gao Village, so that you can share the gospel. They have been praying and fasting for you for three days.'"

In another place he went to preach God had prepared the people in a quite extraordinary way. It was in Fen Shuiling village in Nanyang. An unbeliever there was dying after a long illness and there was no hope. His family had never heard the gospel but one evening Jesus came to the sick man's room and physically appeared to him and said, "My name is Jesus. I have come to save you."

Brother Yun, says, "The Fen Shuiling village is situated in a remote mountainous area where preachers had not yet visited with the gospel. It had no church or pastor, so when I visited there I was surprised to find the gospel had spread to many villages and that dozens of families had put their faith in Christ. These new believers were now hungry to receive teaching from God's Word."

Jesus Himself had preached the gospel to them!

19

NORMAN CAMPBELL

The Hebridean Revival in Scotland, 1949-1952

The above photo is of the Church of Scotland in Barvas on the Isle of Lewis where the last recorded revival in the British isles took place. The man whose name is synonymous with this powerful move of God in 1949 is Duncan Campbell who was invited to the Island to preach for a short series of meetings and stayed for three years. On one occasion he was billed as 'the man who brought revival to Lewis.' He was extremely upset by that and made it clear on many occasions that, 'I did not bring revival to Lewis. Revival was already in

Lewis before I came. I thank God that I had the privilege of being there, and, in some small measure leading the movement for about three years, but God moved in the parish of Barvas before I ever set foot on the Island.'

The present minister of the church is a good friend of mine and a few years ago I had the privilege of speaking with some of the older members. They recalled with tears in their eyes and awe in their voice the mighty things God did in those days. Duncan Campbell described it as a community saturated with God. The outstanding characteristic of the revival on the Island was 'The conscious presence of the Lord.'

Norman Campbell (no relation of Duncan) tells of his conversion to Christ at this time.

"One night during the movement of the Spirit in our corner of the Island, both Rev MacLennan and Rev Campbell were in the pulpit together. Mr MacLennan was deeply moved and his face was white as he challenged us with the words applicable to many of us, he said, 'You are here tonight, but there was a time when you were in the stern of a ship praying to the Lord and promising Him that if He would get you out of here alive, you would follow Him and serve Him. Have you kept your promise? What are you going to do tonight?

I remembered that I had been on the *California*. It was a passenger boat at the time and we were put in the stern of the ship. There were about forty men from Lewis in the crew. Some of them prayed. One young fellow had his Bible and he would kneel to pray. It came back to me at the close of that meeting when God spoke to many souls.

Mr Campbell then asked for those who wished to be prayed for, to join him in the church hall. I joined the others who were seeking help. Mr Campbell and I knelt together and he prayed. He then asked me to pray and ask the Lord for mercy. As soon as I stood to pray, my chains were loosed and I was set free. I left the hall feeling as if I were swimming in a sea of love... All I wanted to do was go to heaven! I was thrilled with the presence of God."

Later that evening Norman tells of another dramatic encounter he had with God.

"After we had a meal we went to the bus, and just as we approached the vehicle, suddenly a light like the brightness of the sun, on this dark night shone around us. I looked up to see where the light was coming from and I saw the face of Christ. That was where the light was coming from – His Face! I shall never forget it! It was like the sun, just like the sun! And the joy on that face; and the love reflected from that face! I cannot explain nor describe it. Then He said, 'I love you.' The vision lasted only a few seconds but it seemed that it was a few minutes. I was simply flooded with inexpressible joy and seemed to be afloat in an ocean of love."

20

DAVID YONGGI CHO

The World's Largest Church

Dr David Yonggi Cho is senior pastor of Yoido Full Gospel Church, the largest church in the world.

Located in Seoul, Korea, the congregation reached 400,000 in 1984, and 700,000 in 1992. In the 1990s, Cho decided that rather than expanding further, the church should establish satellite churches in other parts of the city. Goals for the decade of 2000-10 include the establishment of 5,000 satellite churches.

In 1976, he founded Church Growth International (CGI) as a forum for sharing his biblical principles of church growth. Participants in CGI seminars number over seven million. He is the author of more than 100 books, and in 1985 received the *Gold Medallion Book Award* from the Evangelical Christian Publisher's Association for his work, *Prayer The Key to Revival*. He has served as the Executive Committee Chairman of the World Assemblies of God Fellowship.

When Cho was growing up he was greatly influenced by and trained in Buddhism, Confucianism and Eastern studies. When he was 17 he suffered from tuberculosis and almost died. His sister's Christian friend frequently visited him, and he accepted Christ as his personal saviour and experienced a remarkable healing in his body. The doctor who had taken X-rays and told Cho that the tuberculosis had ravaged his body and would soon kill him within three months was dumbfounded when new X-rays were taken. He told Cho, "I don't know where it went or what happened, but there is no evidence that your body has ever had TB. Not only that, but your heart seems to be normal size, whereas before, it was abnormally enlarged. This is a medical wonder! You are a new man!"

Cho made up his mind to study medicine and become a doctor to help the needs of his people who were suffering greatly. He threw himself into his studies and caring for the sick but it was to take a great toll on his own health and strength. During this time he made the wholehearted commitment to live his life solely for Christ and became the interpreter for an American evangelist. He also began to study the Bible and believe God for a total and complete miracle for his health which had again began to trouble him.

One day he locked the door of his room and began to pray. "Mister Jesus, I want to meet you and have a consultation about my future." He waited and nothing happened. He prayed all day, and by nighttime he was soaked in perspiration. Finally, tired and exhausted, his body gave in to sleep.

He awoke a few hours later after midnight hungry from not having eaten all day. "Okay, Mister Jesus, I'm ready to pray some more," he continued, praying in the politest way he knew how. "Sir, I am quite hungry and it's late at night; if you can recreate my lungs then you must also be able to supply noodles to soothe the hunger pains in my stomach." Continuing with his eyes closed tight and trying to remember everything he had been taught about prayer and how to pray, he was startled to hear a loud knock on his door. Dressed in a white uniform and a white hat, a delivery boy handed him a red and gold lacquer box from the nearby Chinese restaurant saying, "I saw your light on and I had one too many on my last run." The boy must also have been startled by Cho looking into his face for a long time without saying a word. Eating the noodles and enjoying the side dish of kimchi that came with them, Cho was now more than wide awake.

The Encounter

Suddenly a smell of smoke filled the air and to his left a cloud of grey smoke bellowed before him. Then startlingly, and at first confusingly, what seemed to look like a fireman appeared in the room. Cho knew he had locked the door after the delivery boy, but now this person stood barefoot on the floor before him, a white robe draping His ankles. Cho glanced upward and his eyes fixed on the face of a man who looked straight into his eyes. From a wound on his forehead there oozed a stain of blood and a wreath of thorns sat upon His head. "My Lord! My Lord!" cried Cho.

Kneeling to Cho's level, the man pointed a finger at him and started talking clearly and distinctly, "Young man, you are ambitious. You are looking for fame and money. I tell you this kingdom will crumble. But I have a kingdom that will not crumble. You are to go out and preach about my kingdom that does not crumble."

Cho reached out to touch Jesus' garment and then gently fell asleep until morning.

When he awoke he felted rested and filled with new power and energy. He went outside and began to tell those he met that there is a kingdom that does not crumble. He said, "Korea has crumbled before – not once but many times. I know a kingdom that does not crumble, and it's not America, not Japan, not Russia, not England, not even China."

Cho's destiny had been decided and it was not to be a medical doctor. He entered the Full Gospel Bible Institute in Seoul.

After Cho left home to attend Bible School, his mother quietly started going to church and was baptised. His father, a learned man in the Eastern religions, made no objection but later blamed her and his eldest son, Cho, for how badly his woollen underwear business was going. So he decided to take a trip to Seoul and have a talk with his wayward son. It was a long journey but he arrived just in time to be taken to the Bible School service. Cho was the preacher's interpreter that day, but excited over seeing his father, he preached what he wanted his dad to hear, not always what the other speaker was saying. He prayed earnestly, "O God, bring salvation to my father. Bring salvation to my father."

When the service was over and everyone had left Cho made his way to his father and saw tears streaming down his face. His father explained what had

happened, "I could hardly look up there because of the man who was stood in the middle behind you and the American."

"In the middle?"

"Yes, that man with blood on His forehead smiled at me and pointed His finger right at me. He was like a strange bright light and I could not keep looking. Every time His light pointed to me, I could see all the shameful things I've ever done and even all the evil thoughts I've ever thought."

"Father," said Cho, "would you like to make all those things vanish and start all over like a baby's heart, pure and undefiled by all these years of life up to now?"

Cho led his dad in a prayer for repentance, confessing his sins to God and receiving forgiveness.

21

DAN BAUMANN

Love Conquers Fear

Dan Baumann and his friend, Glenn Murray, spent two exciting weeks sharing the Gospel in Iran during January 1997. Leaving the country they were detained at the border checkpoint and their passports taken. Six hours later the guards returned to say there was a problem with their documents, so Baumann and his friend Glenn Murray were separated, interrogated and beaten for the next six hours as guards kicked and punched them. They were then put in prison clothes, blindfolded and led to separate cells in the basement of a prison block.

So began a nightmarish captivity that both men hoped would end quickly. As Dan sat down on the threadbare carpet opposite the prison door trying to control the conflicting emotions that coursed through him he thought surely it was all a big mistake and the American or Swiss embassies would have him and Glenn out of there in a day at most, or would they? Doubts soon took control and slowly he felt the crippling nausea of hopelessness mixed with fear as desperation began to creep up from the pit of his stomach. He says, "I was locked up alone in the basement of some jail in a country not known for its kindness to strangers, especially Americans like me. And even more disturbing, I had absolutely no idea why I was being held captive."

As he lay in his cell hot tears began to run down his face and he called out to God, "Why did you allow this to happen to me?" There was no answer. Again he cried out in despair, "How long am I going to be here?" Much to his surprise, a voice inside his head spoke. "You will be in here for nine weeks."

Later he discovered he was being held in the infamous Evin prison. It was reserved for the most dangerous political prisoners. It meant he was considered a danger to the country and that he could be held there for a very long time.

He was put in a cell with a light in one corner that was on 24 hours a day. It was wintertime with snow on the ground outside but the heater in the cell didn't work well. As the waiting dragged on, he started to fear that he would just waste away in prison in Iran without anyone knowing why he was there. He says there was no sense of feeling God's presence as He felt far away, but all he could trust in was the character of God that no matter how he felt or what his circumstances God was faithful.

Almost every day he was taken to be beaten and viciously interrogated. They led him down a hallway to the interrogation room, which was very dark and murky with bloodstains on the floor. The beatings would start as they slapped his face, punched him in the stomach and sometimes kicked him.

After two weeks he hit rock bottom. Day fourteen was to be the lowest point of his prison experience but it also became one of the greatest experiences of his life. He says, "I became even more pessimistic about ever being released. I began torturing myself with depressing thoughts: I'm an American in a country where the United States is referred to as the 'great satan' who am I kidding? They are never going to let me go."

Then he says he heard a voice inside his head say, "Come on home Dan. Everything will be okay, just come on home." He recognized the voice as that of an old friend who had died a year before. Then a second voice spoke into his mind, "Yeah, Dan, come on up. You'll love it here." This time it was the voice of his best friend from college who had died at twenty nine after becoming sick on a mission trip to Africa.

Looking around his cell one thought dominated him, how could he kill himself and go to be with them. Things became so bad all he wanted to do was die and be free from his torment and be with Jesus. He was convinced God had allowed his friends to talk to him so that he would not be afraid to kill himself. However, committing suicide would not be easy as the guards had made sure there was nothing sharp within his cell, but then his eyes rested on the sink on the far wall where he thought he could drown himself. He could plug the sink with his shirt and tie one end of his towel to the left bracket and the other end loosely to the right bracket which secured the sink. Once he put his head into the water he would pull the towel into a tight knot that he could not untie even if he wanted to. In fact if his plan worked any struggling on his part would only tighten the towel that much more, making it impossible for him to escape.

With the “invitation” from his two friends still ringing in his ears, he tied one end of the towel to the bracket and waited for the guard to do his rounds and check on him. Immediately after this Dan pulled off his prison pyjama jacket and plugged the sink. He filled it with water and stuck his head under for a couple of pre runs. The sensation of gasping for air was a horrible one but it was the only way out. He took the loose end of the towel and wrapped it around the right bracket twice. Without thinking about it or trying to draw one last deep gasp of air he plunged his head into the sink. The water was cold against his face and he reached for the end of the towel pulling it and forcing his head further into the sink. As he prepared to loop the towel around the bracket one last time to knot it firmly in place, his hands began to tremble violently releasing the towel and allowing him to lift his head to breath.

He collapsed to the floor, gasping for air and twenty minutes passed before he stopped coughing up water and began to breath normally again. He was disappointed his suicide attempt had failed but he knew it would work the next time if he resolved to stop his hands from shaking. He thought again of his college friend’s words as he thrust his head into the water determined to go all the way this time. He was just about to pull the knot tight and trap his head under the water when something broke inside him. Once again he released the tension on the towel and collapsed to the floor. His body was racked with deep uncontrollable sobs. He realized what he was attempting was wrong and the thoughts he had were not from his deceased friends. He realized they had come from Satan who wanted to destroy his life.

As he sat slumped on the cell floor he cried out for God to forgive him. He said, “The only place I am safe is in your presence. I will stay in prison the rest of my life if that is where you want me. But I promise that no matter whatever happens, I will never try to kill myself again. I know it's not the way you have for me to get out of this place. I will walk the path you have made for me and try not to make my own way. Amen."

There in his brokenness and shame suddenly light and glory filled the cell. He wondered what was happening and as he turned around he saw Jesus with a smile on His face. Dan says, "At my lowest point he met me. He looked at me and said, 'Dan, I love you and I promise to carry you through this time.'"

The next day Dan was so excited he could barely stand it. He picked up his Bible and looking down saw it opened at the book of Daniel 10. His eyes fell on verse twelve and thirteen, *"Do not be afraid, Daniel. Since the first day you set your mind to gain understanding and humble yourself before God, your words were heard, and I have come in response to them. But the Prince of Persian kingdom resisted me twenty one days. Then Michael, one of the chief princes, came to help me, because I was detained the with the king of Persia."*

It had been exactly twenty one days since Dan's passport had been taken from him and now he knew beyond a shadow of a doubt that God had allowed him to be in prison for a purpose. Throughout the rest of the day he reread that passage many times, and with each reading, hope welled up within him.

After this his attitude changed towards the other prisoners and the guards. He says, God challenged me about love for our enemies. He asked me how I felt about my interrogator, the man who beat me and seemed to hate me the most. I began to see God's love for this man and how He loved him and cared about him and his family. The next time I saw my interrogator I said to him, "Sir, if I am going to see you the rest of my life, every day, then why don't we become friends?" He said to me, "That is impossible." I said, "Sir, You can start by telling me your name." I stretched out my hand and said, "Let's be friends." He just froze and after a few minutes he stretched out his hand towards mine and he shook my hand with tears running down his face and said, "My name is Razzak, and I would love to be your friend.'"

Later Dan heard the guards talking about him and his friend saying that they were Christians and follow Jesus. Another said, "These foreigners knew they would have problems when they came here but they have come to us, they have a reason to live and a reason to die." Three of the guards said they were going to follow Jesus. One of them later protected Dan from a warden who tried to kill him. When the warden was asked why he wanted to kill Baumann he told his colleagues, "I don't know what happens to me. Everything is fine during the day, but at night I want to kill him. Every night at about ten or eleven o'clock a dark force seems to enter me. It takes me over and makes me do things. It gets inside my head. I know it's something to do with demons. When I was younger I first encountered the power of demons which I allowed to enter me to give me power. When this foreigner came to the prison I felt a strong demon say to me, 'I want to live inside you because there is someone in this prison I want to destroy.'"

The following night at 1am the warden came to Dan's cell ranting and raving that he was going to kill him. One of the guards who had befriended Dan and accepted Christ spoke out the name of Jesus which caused the warden to give out a blood curdling scream and run away. Over the next two nights the same thing happened seven or eight more times until finally it was over when the warden told the guards he no longer wanted to kill the prisoner and never wanted to harm him and was now going to do all he could to help him.

Dan's friend Glenn was released after five weeks but exactly nine weeks not only to the day but to the hour, which God had told him at the start of his imprisonment, Dan was released by Iran's high court.

Dan continues to travel the world sharing the amazing love and power of God.

Group Encounters

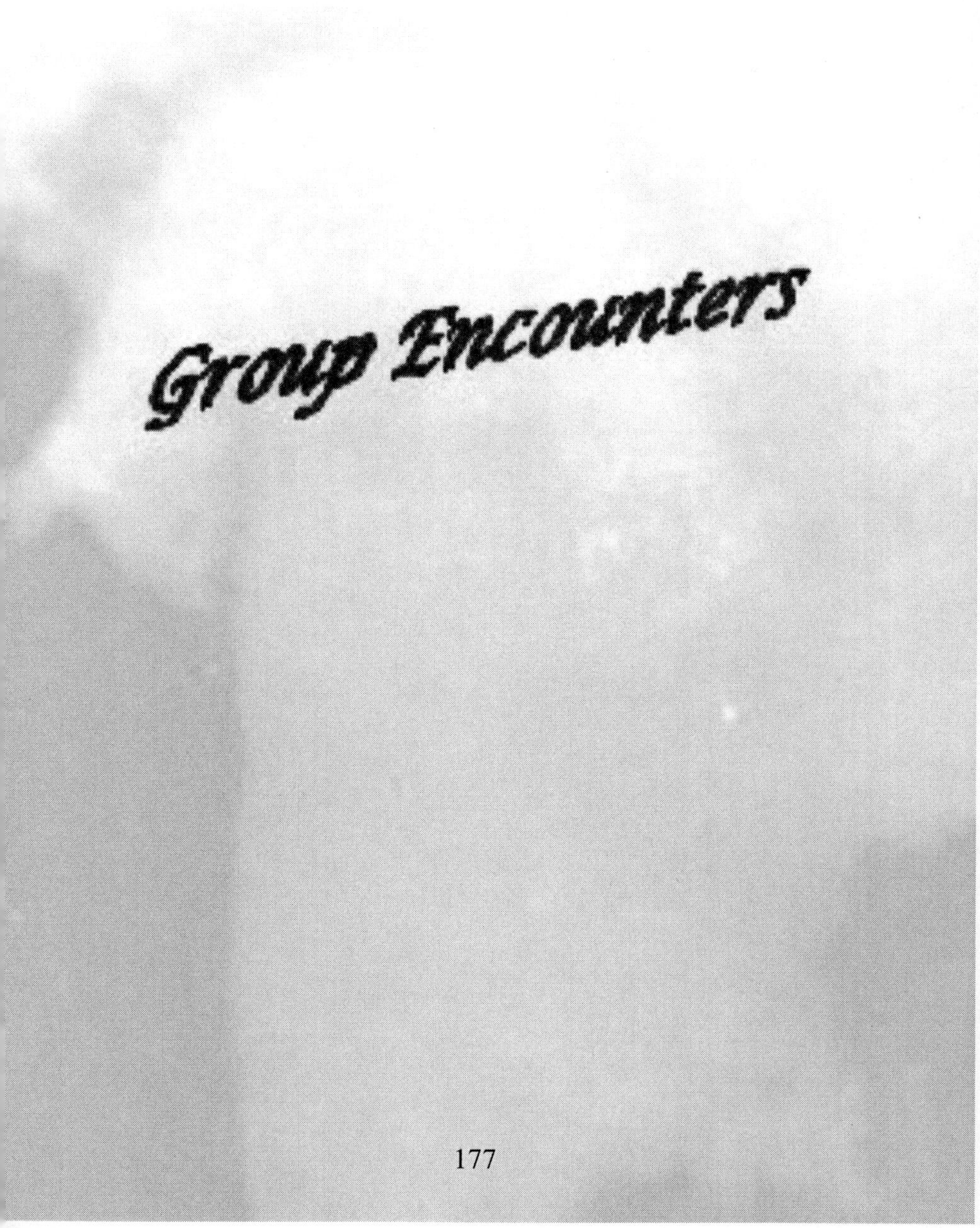

22

STEPHEN JEFFREYS

An Awesome Vision

Born and raised in the valleys of South Wales, Stephen Jeffreys went to work in the coal mines at the age of 12. He led a typical mining lifestyle until 1904 when the great Welsh Revival invaded those mines. For several days he was under deep conviction of sin. Other men working with him had been converted. Finally he came to Christ and became a totally changed man, he was aged 28. Immediately he started attending all the local prayer meetings and especially all open air meetings. He soon began preaching with great fire and passion. He continued working in the mines for several years but at every opportunity he preached in the open air.

Eventually the time came when both he and his wife Elizabeth were convinced that God was calling him into fulltime ministry as an evangelist.

He received an invitation from a Baptist church in Llanelli, Wales, to conduct an evangelistic campaign and this proved so successful it continued for several weeks. Afterwards he decided to stay in the town and opened a church of his own in a building which for some obscure reason was called Island Place and in seven of the happiest years of his ministry he made it world famous.

The most amazing thing that took place during this time happened on the first Sunday night in July, 1914 as he preached on the text *"That I may know him, and the power of his resurrection and the fellowship of his sufferings,"* Philippians 3:10. Jeffreys said he was conscious of a tremendous anointing and extra power and blessing and he could see the people were riveted in his direction. As soon as he had finished speaking his wife beckoned him to come down from the pulpit and then he saw the reason for the remarkable affect upon the congregation – there on the wall behind the pulpit was a vision of Christ for all to see.

A lady called Mrs Harris Williams who had been sitting next to Mrs Jeffreys in the service, said, "Just behind our dear pastor there appeared the head of a lamb with two horns. Then, as I was trying to get Mrs Jeffreys to see it, the head became a face with two beautiful tears rolling down. The pastor was appealing to sinners and the beautiful face of the Man of Sorrows was enshrouded with glory."

Stephen Jeffreys recounted what happened next,

"When I came down among the congregation and looked where I had been, there in the wall was the living face of Jesus, His hair was like wool parted in the middle. When I examined closer it looked as though His hair was streaked with white like that of a middle aged man in grief. We remained in the chapel for a long time looking and scores of others who heard about it came to examine. Among them was a strong skeptic, who declared, 'I have seen and now I believe.' He came in an infidel and went out a believer."

Hundreds flocked to see the sight, which remained for several hours. Some actually tried to erase the face but failed to do so. One man John Richards, a painter and decorator testified, "With my handkerchief in my hands I went and placed it over the object. Then imagine my surprise to find that object shining through my handkerchief."

Another lady in the congregation, Mrs Every, declared, "The chapel was very full. Between eight and nine o'clock I saw my Saviour's face distinctly on the wall. His eyelids flickered quite clearly. A Man of Sorrows – so He appeared. At the close of the meeting it was still there for several more hours."

Skeptics who came in were not slow to make their suggestions. One said it was some kind of hallucination caused by the flickering of a light. A witness said, "The pastor did not stop to argue that the electric light was not flickering but turned it out at once and there, more clearly shining, living and real, was our Saviour. Not to be beaten the skeptic argued that it must be projected by some kind of optical apparatus through a window from outside. Then the pastor had all the blinds drawn and that made no difference whatsoever, for the vision was just the same."

The vision was thoroughly investigated and all but the most obdurate accepted it as a sign from God. For many years there was no shortage of dependable eye witnesses to confirm its genuineness. The Vicar of Wall near Litchfield, Rev JW Adams MA, twice visited Llanelli, first in 1926 and again the following year. He questioned many eye witnesses and listed over a score of people with their names and addresses who were all ready to confirm the story.

The caretaker of Island Place, Robert John Williams, in his account said, “I looked at the face from all angles but which ever way I looked His eyes seemed to follow me everywhere. I stayed there for some time, so I am quite sure of what I saw. The crowd became so great that I locked the place up. After going about a mile on my way home I decided to return. The vision was still there, exactly the same as when I left. My wife and daughters saw exactly the same as I did.”

Jeffreys prayed to know the meaning of this strange and wonderful happening. He said, “I thought the vision was granted for something more than emphasising my sermon. After I had prayed to know its meaning it seemed to be a sign of terrible suffering about to come but I did not know what. Then a fortnight later, when war began, I knew what it was and ever since have recognised it as a sign of the beginning of the end of this age.”

Numerous newspapers carried the story. The first record is found in the *Llanelly and County Guardian* of July 9. Other reports are found in the *Llanelly Argus* July 11, where it appeared on the front page with the heading, “Miracles and Mysteries, Island Place Mission, A Strange Story.” *The South Wales Press* ran a similar account on July 15 and the *Llanelly Mercury* a day later.

The most detailed account we have is recorded in *Confidence,* the first Pentecostal magazine in Britain. It reported an interview by the editor, Alexander Boddy, with Stephen Jeffreys and was printed in July 1916. Jeffreys had been preaching at the National Pentecostal Convention held in Westminster Central Hall, London, at Whitsun. He spoke about the story of Peter on the Mount of Transfiguration (Matthew 17:1-8). The report was headed, ***“The Face of Christ – A Miraculous Appearance. Has it any reference to the War?”***

It read, "At the London Convention on Tuesday, June 13, at the evening meeting Brother Stephen Jeffreys (the Collier-Preacher of South Wales) was speaking and referring to 'Mountain-Top Experiences.'

"He told us in the course of his sermon in the Central Hall how, when he was preaching in Wales nearly two years ago, there came suddenly a supernatural picture upon the wall above the platform. At first it was the head of a lamb, then it gradually changed and became the face of the Man of Sorrows.

"There it remained in the sight of the congregation and of everyone who came in to see it. It was as just a little while before the commencement of the Great War. It was surely in some way a warning as to that terrible thing that was coming on the earth.

"I had a talk with our Brother after the meeting. Mr George Every ("Springfield," Westbury Street, Llanelly, South Wales) was standing with us, and he corroborated as an eye-witness all that Pastor Stephen Jeffreys said.

"Will you let me ask you some questions as to this miraculous picture of Christ?" I said. "Yes, gladly I will," he replied.

"First, exactly where did it appear?"

"On the wall of the Island Place Mission Room at Llanelly (South Wales) above the platform."

"Was it at night and during a meeting?

"Yes, I was preaching, and I noticed that the people were all beginning to look at something behind me, and at last I stopped and turned to see what it was that attracted their attention, and then saw the face."

"What kind of light was there in that hall?"

"It was lit by electric light. Everything was quite plain."

"What was the wall like? Was it plastered? Had it a smooth surface?"

"It was something like the wall over there. Tinted, or slightly coloured."

"Could you go today and put your hand on the wall exactly where it appeared?"

"Indeed I could. It was there for six hours, to be seen by everyone. Next day it had gone."

"Did anyone try to explain it?"

"No, no one could possibly explain it. It was just there for everyone to see, above the platform. It was a vision sent to us by the Lord. It reminded us that He was indeed the slain Lamb, and that that Lamb was identical with the crucified saviour bearing the sin of the world. He seemed to be sorrowing with His people over the things which were coming upon the earth."

"Brother Every said that he went up to the wall and was close to the picture. It was the size of a man's face. The eyes were remarkable, they seemed to be alive and moving. (He drew as it were with his finger on the wall where we were standing the shape and size of the picture.) I asked Brother Every if he could send me any account which had appeared in one of the local papers. He has sent me the following cutting from the *Llanelly Star*:

"A remarkable experience is related by those who attend the mission services now being held at the Island Place Gospel Hall. For some months past Mr Stephen Jeffreys, an earnest mission worker, has been conducting services here among a section of the community to whom the churches and chapels seem to make no appeal. During the service on Sunday night the congregation were startled to see a vision appearing on the wall behind where the preacher was standing. The outlines appeared to be blurred at first, but by-and-by the congregation recognised the head and face of the Man of Sorrows, with the crown of thorns upon His head.

"Speaking to a *Star* representative today, Mr Jeffreys gave a thrilling account of what he described as 'The vision of the Master.'

"'We have had many conversions,' he said, 'but what occurred on Sunday night transcends all that one could have hoped for. My back was turned to the portion of the wall where the vision appeared, and my attention was drawn to it by some of the congregation who were spell -bound to see the face of our Blessed Lord standing boldly out on the wall. There was no mistaking the appearance. It was the Man of Sorrows looking on us with ineffable love and compassion shining out of His wonderful eyes.

"'The effect upon us all was one that will never be forgotten by any who were privileged to behold it. Some of my congregation saw the head crowned with thorns, but I cannot speak as to this as I did not see it. The face, however, was not to be mistaken, and it still haunts me. It remained on the wall for hours after the service closed, and we kept the building open in order that all should have the opportunity of witnessing this wonderful revelation.

"'Many unbelievers came in and fell on their knees in penitence. It was a proof to us that the Lord is with us in our work, and it will inspire us to more wholehearted consecration to His service.'

"Brother Every secured for *Confidence* a copy of a photo taken shortly afterwards, showing the spot (marked with X) where the picture appeared."

THE LONDON CONVENTION. Page 111.

JULY, 1916. VOL. IX. No. 7.

"CONFIDENCE"

EDITED BY

ALEX. A. BODDY,

ALL SAINTS' VICARAGE, SUNDERLAND, ENGLAND.

PICTURE-VISION OF CHRIST.

The X marks the place on the wall where it appeared in Island Place Mission, Llanelly, So. Wales. (Bro Stephen Jeffreys in the Rostrum.) Page 113.

"This is the CONFIDENCE that we have in Him, that if we ask anything according to His will, He heareth us. And if we know that He hear us, whatsoever we ask, we know that we have the petitions that we desired from Him."—*1 John v., 14-15.*

100th ISSUE.

ONE PENNY.

London: Samuel E. Roberts, Publisher, Zion House, 5a, Paternoster Row, E.C.

"CONFIDENCE EDITED BY ALEX. A. BODDY, No, 7. Vol. ix.
ALL SAINTS', SUNDERLAND, July, 1916.

23

JESUS APPEARS IN ARABIA

Christine Darg is the founder of *Exploits Ministry,* which ministers powerfully throughout the Middle East and the Islamic nations. Along with her husband, Peter, she also established the *Christian Broadcasting Network's* news bureau in Jerusalem. In her fascinating book *Miracles among Muslims* she records the amazing account of Jesus' physical appearance to a classroom of Muslim students in a school in Arabia. It happened on February 19, 1994, and has been carefully documented. These children, whose parents were expatriates, represented many Muslim nations. They have now gone back to their homelands with a message and experience that will reach out to many.

Darg says she was invited to hold meetings at this school not long after this event had taken place. There was a tremendous outpouring of the Holy Spirit and the presence of God. There were many salvations while she ministered there particularly amongst the staff, and especially the men, who sat, to begin with arms rigidly folded across their chests, in the back of the hall. Some attended the revival meetings only because their presence was compulsory. These schoolmasters were rigid and unyielding – until the Holy Ghost fell upon them with convicting revival fire! Some of the men were new staff masters who had never experienced the previous visitation of God, let alone spiritual rebirth! Graciously, the Holy Spirit broke down their hardness or uncertainties, and they began to shake with conviction of sin and many came to faith in Jesus Christ.

Because of the political and religious climate in this region Darg sensibly does not give out all the details regarding the exact location and name of the school. She does, however, give us a great deal of other detail with first hand testimonies of what actually happened on that extraordinary day when Jesus visited the children's classroom.

The Physical Appearance of Jesus

The following song was composed by a 10-year-old Muslim boy named Sulman and was taught to his fellow classmates. It was this cry for God that the children were singing when Jesus appeared to them simultaneously;

I Am Blessed

I am blessed,
I am blessed everyday of my life, I am blessed.
When I wake up in the morning
And as I lay my head to rest,
I am blessed,
I am blessed.
More of you, more of you,
Thirsty I cry,
God hear my cry I need more of you.

As the boys stood singing the beautiful words, "More of you...thirsty I cry," on a February morning during Ramadan,

Jesus entered the school to answer that cry. The large window of the corner classroom gently wafted with clouds, and then brilliant golden rays penetrated and finally shaped into the "beautiful," "strange," "special person." He held an "old book" with golden edges. They saw that the book was embossed with "HB," standing for Holy Bible.

The students called the visitor's garment a white "*kandura*" (robe). Many testified that, "They saw Him as three; but did not know which of the three He was, but saw Him again as one." The encounter only lasted a few minutes but each boy felt that the Lord was personally beside him, touching him.

All the children simultaneously saw, heard and felt the close proximity of His divine presence, describing His loving, beautiful and awesome presence, beyond description, with a golden, radiant light around His head, yet worn sandals on His feet. But as He walked around the class, wherever His feet moved, there were sparks of silver and gold.

More than one of the children reported that His presence brought the fragrance of "roses" or "flowers."

The Children's Testimonies

"A day I will never forget"
By M. Sulman from Dares Salaam, Tanzania

February 19, 1994, was the most wonderful day of my life. I was praying in the morning and I saw a gentleman just up in the sky. I got shocked but when he came closer to the ground, I saw him becoming three men, and I couldn't understand which was the real man. He just entered the classroom's window like a ghost. I was nearly about to faint but, in this man, there was something different. When he saw me he was smiling. Then he was coming nearer and nearer. First I got scared so much, but this time my heart was not beating fast. It was filled with happiness. As he was walking the same thing happened – he was becoming three and again becoming one, again three and again one. Now I saw that he was holding a very old book in his hand.

This time was the most important time when he came and stood near me. I was very, very, very scared. But when I felt his soft hand touch my head, it was like as if pure heavenly waters were running across my body. Then he asked me for my wishes. First I thought of games and play and to enjoy life. Then I thought once more. The final exam was coming closer. Then I told him my wishes without fear, which I wanted to pass the final exam. He touched my head and said, "It is done." I didn't want to blink my eyes even for a second because he was so beautiful that I wanted to look and look and look at him. But my teacher could not see him. We told her he was touching her head, but she did not know it. Later I passed the exam. Now when I am not scared of this man, he no more comes to see me, but only visits me in my prayer and dreams. If I need something, he gives it to me. I will never forget him.

"My very strange experience"
By M. Zakin from Zaire

The date in which this strange thing happened was on February 19, 1994, I saw a shot of golden light coming towards us. It became more and more bigger. At last I saw that it became a streak of light, and it came in the class and dashed on the walls. Then it came behind the class. Just then a man appeared with a long white dress. It was something like a *kandura* and had a green cloth on one side. He even wore old sandals. He was so tall that he almost touched the ceiling. He looked very handsome. He was very fair and had curly hair.

He brought a book with letters H.B. He wore a golden bangle on his head. He was very beautiful.

He went around the class and touched everybody's head. When he came near me, I got a nice smell of rose flowers. Teacher was very angry with our class because we made much noise. She did not see him, but we all saw him touch her on her head. When I went home I was thinking and thinking about this. I felt like fever. My parents asked me what had happened, and I told them. They, too, didn't believe me, like teacher. They took me to the mosque, and we met the mullah. I told him everything. He said that *Issa Nabie* (Jesus the Prophet) had visited us, and it is for good. So we were all happy. I know you feel it is hard to believe it, but whatever I saw is very true. He gave me all my wishes. He said, "It is done." I often think about this strange experience.

"An Unforgettable experience"
By I. Iqbal and I. Rashid from Sudan

It was February 19, 1994. We were praying as usual, when something happened. We could see the window and to our surprise, we saw black clouds. Then a moment later a streak of light just passed through the window. It bounced off a wall and landed at the back of the class. We were astonished to see a man at the back of the class. He was a very tall man almost reaching to the top of the ceiling. He had fair, brown, curly hair, and was wearing a long white dress with a green cloth. He was wearing old worn-out sandals with a big golden ring on top of his head. He was so strange, but so handsome. He had in his hand one old leather book with H.B. letters. He went around and touched everyone's head. Our teacher entered the class, and he touched her head also. The teacher was angry with us because we shouted, "Teacher, the man is touching you!" She did not know anything that was going on. As the prayer finished, he disappeared.

"A thrilling experience in my school life" *By M. Farook from Egypt*

I was praying in class on February 19, 1994. It was a beautiful day, and suddenly dark clouds appeared in the sky and a streak of light came through the window and bounced on the walls several times and stopped. And I saw a man, very tall, touching the ceiling. He was very fair with brown curly hair touching his shoulders. He was wearing a white *kandura* with a green cloth. He was carrying an old book with a golden border with something like H.B. written on it. I saw a bangle on his head, and he asked us for three wishes. I told him my wish. I wanted to become first or second in the class. But I became fourth. I felt cold water running through my heart when he touched me. He touched teacher, but she did not feel it. He disappeared as we finished the prayer.

"A day I cannot forget" *By Ibne from Morocco*

We were praying in a classroom on February 19. Our window was black. Actually, outside the window there were some black clouds. Then a streak of light dashed on the wall, and because of that streak of light, we could not see what it was. A boy in our class became momentarily blind. A man appeared from the streak of light. He was a tall man almost touching the ceiling. He was fair with brown, curly hair. He wore a long, white dress with a green cloth and old sandals. He had an old leather book with a gold border. H.B. was written on it. He went around touching our heads and asked for three wishes. I felt like cold water was flowing through my heart. We told our wishes. The man had a golden light on his head. He was looking very nice. I felt like I was in the air. He granted my wishes. He touched teacher also. Teacher said she didn't know what we were saying to her. The man disappeared. Suddenly after the prayer finished, the boy who could not see could now see. This day is a very strange day I will never forget.

"A strange day"
By Amin from Egypt

We were praying in the morning on February 19, 1994. Then we saw dark clouds outside the window. Then it bounced on the window very slowly, and then it stood at the back of the class. We were still praying. My friend could not see him, and another could not talk. Then one friend turned back to see that everyone was praying. Then he saw three men becoming one. He came in front slowly, and he touched everyone's head and said, "What are the three wishes you want?" First I asked him for video games, and then I asked him to make me pass in the exam that was coming near. I got a higher position in the class for the first time. He wore a *kandura* and his hair was brown and curly, and it reached to shoulder level. He had a round, golden bangle, and he held the Holy Bible. He went and golden footsteps were on the ground. Then our prayer finished, and he disappeared. I told my parents, but they did not believe me at first, but after sometime they said, "It's a miracle."

"The memorable day of my life"
By M. Shoboh from Tanzania

It was February 19, 1994. We were praying. Suddenly, outside there was a black cloud with thunder. Then a streak of light, and it just passed through the window. The streak hit the walls at the back of the classroom, and it appeared to take the form of a man. Each and every step he took there below on the ground were silver sandal prints. He was very tall with curly hair. He wore a *kandura* and a green shawl. He looked very handsome. I felt as if he was a stranger. His sandals were worn out. I closed my eyes in terror. Suddenly, when I opened my eyes, I saw him near me. I was very afraid. My friend and I were leading the prayer. He had an old, leather book with a gold border. He had a bangle above his head. Suddenly, he touched me and asked me for three wishes. I saw him touching teacher and my friend, but only my friend saw him. Teacher could not see him or feel him. That time we were singing the song, “I am blessed.”

"The visit (a memorable day)"
By Rasool from Sudan

In the morning of February 19, 1994, during the morning prayer, I had a strange experience. I had prayed once before with my friends, but that morning when I was praying with my friends at 8:15am. I heard someone talking to me. I could not open my eyes but I felt strange. I knew someone big was standing very close to me. I could feel it. He urged me to say in my prayer what I needed. At first I thought, who is this guy, what does he want? But he had a strong voice, and I obeyed. As I had asked, a day later, my brother was born and in that trimester exam, I got the first place. My friends said that they saw him. They also said to me that he talked to almost everyone. The visitor was different from all others. Something was special about him. I felt so very happy. It was a memorable day, and I can't forget this incident, most of all the visitor, because my wishes were said in the prayer, and they came true. I think he is a saint.

"The day I cannot forget"
By Ahmed from Somalia

That was the most wonderful day in my life. We were praying on February 19, 1994. I saw dark clouds outside the window. Suddenly, I saw a streak of light enter our class through our window. The streak of light passed through the eyes of my friend. The streak hit the blackboard and went at the back of the class. I was the first one to see him. I was too afraid and turned my face away. My friend tried to ask me what I was doing – but I couldn't answer. The stranger was very handsome and tall. He had a white robe and a green coat over him and had a gold circle on his head. He had a book which was old and asked our wishes. He said our wishes were granted. He even touched our teacher's head and asked her wishes. When he touched mine, I felt cold water flowing through my heart. Each step he took there was a golden light on the floor. After we finished our prayer, we couldn't find him. I wish to see him again.

"A day I will never forget"
By S. Falah from Dares Salaam

Our class was praying during the month of February. It was Ramadan. The date was February 19. Soon we saw dark clouds and from the window a flash of light came and banged the wall. A man appeared from the clouds. The man was tall – touching the ceiling, and he was fair. He had curly hair. The colour of his hair was brown. He had a piece of green cloth on his shoulder. He was wearing a white *kandura*. He kept an old book in his hand. It had a leather cover with a gold border with H.B., and there was also a king's name on it. A golden bangle was on his head. He was handsome and beautiful. He came around and asked us three wishes. I felt like ice water falling on me when he touched me. There was a flower smell in the class. I told him my wishes, and they were granted. I told him to bless my parents, brothers and friends. He touched our teacher. We shouted, "Teacher, the man is touching you," but she asked, "What man?" She didn't see him. After the prayer was finished, we didn't see him.

Comments by Mrs George, The school headmistress

"This vision has opened in a keen way the inward eye of our faith, that is the faith of more than a hundred teachers who are working in an institution brooded over by God's glory in a city of the Arabian Peninsula. It has now led to a new ministry *Vivit, Vivit* (which in Latin means, 'He is alive! He is alive!')

"Yes, now we are excited! For deep down in our heart, our faith is firmly rooted, and we now know for sure that the mighty name of Jesus is not a mere name in history. He is not the man that was. Jesus is not just the landmark of time as history honours Him by the use of AD (Anno Domino) or BC (Before Christ) but He is the God that *was*, that *is*, and that *will be*. He is alive. Yes, He rose from the dead, and His mighty presence is with us, so close that we can hear His heartbeat of abundant love and concern. We can sense His love and feel the warm vibration of His eternal love.

"We teachers are all touched by the power of this mighty vision, so blessedly given to 21 innocent 10-year-old Muslim children. Ever since, our lives have been changed. We no longer mess our lives with the temporary passing desires of this world: *We want, we desire, we thirst now* only for one thing in our life – our Lord. We seek Him continuously; we read the Bible, the Holy Book we teachers knew from our childhood.

"But now it gives a new vision, a new anointing, and a new wisdom to know Him better, to love Him better, and to serve Him better. We want to avoid all sinful habits, for we dare not grieve our divine Holy Lord. We do not want to be separated from Him, for now we know the danger of this separation causes oppression by the evil one."

The classroom where this encounter took place is now set aside for prayer as a chapel to seek the Lord's face. It is significant that the headmistress, Mrs George, had been crying out to God for many months before the visitation occurred. Mrs George is a born-again believer, but she was desperate in her heart for personal revival, to know more of the power of God. Her constant prayer had been, "Jesus, let me see your face!" Her prayer was answered beyond her wildest imaginations, when the Lord showed His face to her Muslim pupils!

Christine Darg

Darg who reported all these events had herself a very dramatic encounter with Jesus. As a very young child, she says she was extremely ill and almost died. She had lost all of her hair, suffered from rheumatic fever and was wasting away.

She recounts,

"One of my earliest childhood memories was the Lord Jesus appearing to me in an open vision. But unlike some Sunday School pictures of a 'Western Jesus,' this Christophany was a Middle Eastern man with long, dark curly hair, brown compassionate eyes and Mediterranean complexion. He was wearing a green and white stripped Biblical robe. From His appearance, He could have been a Jewish King or a

Middle Eastern sheik; He was definitely Semitic. I believe He knew that I would one day live in the Bible lands. He said with warm compassion, 'You are going to be healed.'

"I was fearful and awed by the vision and momentarily turned my head to the side. When I looked again, He was gone, but I was healed! To this day I am blessed with vigorous health and travel throughout the world for Jesus!"

24

CALIFORNIA AND CHINA

California

In his book *Visions of Jesus,* Phillip Wiebe tells of a remarkable vision and encounter with Jesus that more than 50 people had at the Pentecostal Holiness Church in Oakland, California.

One Sunday night in April 1954, the minister, Kenneth Logie was preaching when at 9.15pm he saw a shadow on the exterior glass doors, made by someone standing outside. He wondered who might be arriving so late in the evening and with that the door opened and Jesus starting walking down the aisle. He turned to the people on one side and then the people on the other smiling as He went. He walked up to the platform where Kenneth was speaking, but instead of walking around the pulpit, He moved right through it. When He placed His hand on the minister's shoulder, Kenneth collapsed to the floor. Jesus then knelt down beside him and spoke to him in another language.

Another incident happened in May 1959 in the same church this time with over 200 witnessing the event. A woman in the congregation described a vision she had when she was in hospital and was thought dead. Mrs Lucero, who was of Catholic background, reported that Jesus appeared to her wearing a clerical robe and told her to have faith in God. Kenneth says that when Mrs Lucero got up to tell her story, she was wearing a black raincoat because the weather had been rainy that day. As she spoke she disappeared from view and in her place stood a figure that was recognised as being Jesus. He wore sandals, a glistening white robe, and had nail prints in His hands – hands that dripped with oil. Virtually everyone present saw Him clearly. There was also a member of the church who had an eight millimeter movie camera and was so overcome by what he saw that he had to place his camera on top of the organ to keep it steady. The effect on those present was electrifying as Jesus stood before them for several minutes before disappearing and Mrs Lucero becoming visible again.

Dr Phillip Wiebe says that he saw the film and spoke with several of those who were present that night,

"The circumstances surrounding the film were described to me in 1965 by Kenneth Logie and his wife, both in a public meeting in Grenfell, Saskatchewan, and in private conversation. I was a young undergraduate at the time, and was not comfortable with the thought of giving the film or the supposed incident any attention. I did not speak in detail with Kenneth about these events again until 1991, by which time his first wife had died. I visited him and the church that summer, and spoke with four or five persons who were present in his church in 1959 when the incident took place. They supported what the minister had said. I naturally wanted to see the film again, primarily to refresh my memory concerning what I had seen twenty six years earlier, and was disappointed to learn that it had been stolen from the apartment in which Kenneth lives. I estimate that there were about two hundred people present in the public meeting in Grenfell when I saw the film. I do not know how often it was shown in public, but my impression is that Kenneth showed it in his church from time to time. The woman involved in the incident, Mrs Lucero, who was already quite old at the time it took place, died a few years later.

"My own memory of the film is that it showed a figure that looked like traditional images of Jesus. The woman in the black raincoat did not appear, to my recollection, evidently because it was not significant enough to attract the attention of the person who held the camera (with whom I have not spoken). My memory of the glistening white robe as well as the outstretched and scarred hands is clear, but I cannot remember any movement of the figure, nor do I remember seeing the full face. Kenneth, who naturally saw the film a number of times, says that the face appeared on the film."

Dr Wiebe goes on to say a lot more about the church and Kenneth Logie and other extraordinary things that were reported to have taken place. He also talked about the still photographs he was shown of images that appeared on the walls of the church.

China

I have before me as I write an amazing article written by Karen Feaver and first printed in *Christianity Today* on May 16, 1994. Feaver was an aide to Virginia Congressman Frank Wolf and took part in a US delegation to Beijing in 1994. Although the trip was political, she found herself enthralled by the people's love for Jesus and the power of God.

In 1950 there were estimated to be just one million evangelical Christians in the whole of China. By 1992 even the State Statistical Bureau of China indicated that there were 75 million Christians in China (Asian Report 197, Oct/Nov 1992, p. 9). Today there are reckoned to be as many as 200 million.

Feaver recorded in her account a meeting of the American Delegation headed by Congressman Chris Smith of New Jersey and including members of Christian Solidarity International with three Chinese ladies. The eldest of the three had just been released from her second prison term for preaching the gospel. During her 110 days of captivity, she was hung upside down and beaten with electrical cords. The other women imprisoned with her were beaten with wire from the waist down. She said that God's presence was so tangible during the torture that, in fact, she felt joyful. "Because of these afflictions, we loved the souls of China more," she told them, "and we prayed for those who were torturing us." Feaver noted that although Congressmen do not normally take notes for themselves, Chris Smith picked up his pen to record personally their daily battle cry; "We go out ready to preach the gospel, ready to go to jail, and ready to die for Jesus' sake."

The women said that wherever their brothers and sisters go and tell others of Jesus miraculous signs and wonders follow. Two of the stories that Feaver highlighted were about a Saul like public security officer who was intent on finding and persecuting believers in Christ. His wife became gravely ill and could not walk or talk and the family spent about 80,000 yuan (£5,000) searching for a cure. The local Christians decided to show the officer forgiveness and went to pray for his wife. She was miraculously healed and she and her husband gave their lives to the Lord. He said to them, "Now I know you Christians are really good people. Before I always persecuted Christians, but now I will tell you if the government wants to harm you."

The other account revolved around a brother sharing the simple message of repentance and faith with a crowd hearing the gospel for the first time, the women said,

"A vision of Jesus walking among them and then suffering on the cross appeared to all gathered. When the teacher told of Jesus rising from the dead, the vision showed Jesus ascending to heaven gloriously. Many of those listening put their faith in Christ."

Encounters Beyond The Veil

25

CHOO THOMAS

Heaven Is So Real

In October 2003, a Korean American by the name of Choo Thomas wrote a book which quickly became an international bestseller and was translated into Korean by David Yonggi Cho, the leader of the world's largest church. The title of the book is *Heaven Is So Real* in which the writer describes a series of amazing encounters with Jesus who she says, took her on seventeen occasions to see the reality of heaven and hell and told her she must write of her experiences. Church leaders who know Choo well have endorsed her as a deeply spiritual woman.

She describes how in February 1994 she saw Jesus while she was worshipping at the Neighborhood Assembly of God in Tacoma, Washington. He was sitting by the pulpit and she says she could see Him as clearly as a real person, except she couldn't see His face. He had silky white hair and was wearing a pure white robe. His person was visible to her for almost five minutes. After seeing Him she says, her body felt on fire with unspeakable joy, and as a result she became wholeheartedly committed to Jesus.

Choo describes another encounter with Jesus which happened on January 19, 1996. She says,

> **"I awoke at 3am. My body was shaking. The Lord's presence was so intense in my bedroom that I shook, perspired and felt very weak for more than an hour. Then I heard something.**
>
> **"I turned my head on the pillow to look in the direction of the sound, and there, all aglow, was a figure dressed in white garments. The radiance that emanated from this unknown visitor was so brilliant that I could not see His face, but in my heart of hearts I knew that I had been blessed with a special visitation from the Lord.**
>
> **"How could this be happening to me? I wondered, as I began to tremble even more violently and weep tears of love and joy. It was the Lord – the Lord of heaven and earth – and He had willingly chosen to visit me in this special way. I felt so humbled by His presence. I could not stop crying.**
>
> **"'My daughter, Choo Nam, I am your Lord, and I want to talk to you. You have been my special daughter for a long time.'**

"The impact of His voice, His words, His message hit me with a supernatural force that left me reeling.

"The Lord spoke once more in His calmly reassuring yet very firm voice,

"'Daughter, you are such an obedient child, and I want to give you special gifts. These gifts are going to serve me greatly. I want you to be happy about these gifts.'

"I knew at that moment God was choosing me to do an important work for Him and that this must become my single -minded purpose. I knew I had nothing to give Him except my heart and my life, and I was willing to do whatever He wanted, to go wherever He wanted. It was a night of commitment, challenge and purpose. My wonderful Lord was beginning to reveal His will to me."

The next day she awoke between 3am and 4am. The anointing of the Lord's presence awakened her and was accompanied again by intense heat.

"I was half asleep, but suddenly the Lord's voice woke me completely, saying, 'Daughter, I am going to visit you many times before this work is done. Therefore, I want you to rest during daytime hours. I have many special plans for you. I will use you in a great way, but it will take awhile to get you ready for the work I've called you to do. You must write down what you hear during each of my visits.'

"The whole experience stunned me, and I was amazed to think that He would visit me again and again. Surely one visit with the Lord should

> **be enough? Yet He said He would be returning to me personally so that He could get me ready for the work He has for me to do.**
>
> **"On January 28 I awoke, shaking again. It was between 2am and 3am in the morning. I felt so overcome by the presence of the Lord that I was weak. My body was so hot that I was perspiring. It seemed as if I was dreaming, but I soon realized that this was no dream.**
>
> **"'I am your Lord, my daughter,' Jesus said. Then I glanced toward the window, in the direction of His majestic voice, and I saw His radiant figure standing there.**
>
> **"'I know you have been so hungry to serve me, but you did not know how to serve me yet. I know you do not want to be embarrassed when you come before me. I know all your thoughts, and I love your thoughts.'"**

A few days later on February 1 Choo says the Lord visited her again at around 11pm.

> **"Immediately the Lord spoke to me, 'My precious daughter, I must show you my presence and talk with you before this work begins.'**
>
> **"His radiant presence had always been stunningly brilliant, but this time He was dressed in white and shining like the sun. His form was beautiful to behold, and so very compelling."**

On March 23 Choo says,

"The Lord came into my room and sat by the window. Then I saw my transformed body sitting next to the Lord, and I was greatly surprised. It was as if I was having a total out-of-the-body experience – I was pure spirit. Jesus' tender voice spoke to me, 'You are living your life completely for me. Your heart has willingly given up all worldly things for me. I now know that nothing brings satisfaction to you more than being in my presence. Therefore, I never want you to say that you are not good enough for me. Your faithfulness is very important to me...'

"Then the Lord showed me His feet and hands. I could see the scars from the nails in His feet and hands...I noticed that the tops of both of His feet had deep round scars on them. Then I looked at His hand – there were round, white scars very close to His wrists...

"People often ask me, 'Were your experiences in heaven like visions or dreams, or did you actually go there?' My only response to these questions is that I know I've seen heaven, and I know that heaven is so real. Whether we place my experiences in the category of supernatural dreams, visions or actual experiences, I will leave to the theologians. All I can say is that they were very real to me...

"Even though I can see the features of my own transformed face quite vividly, I cannot see the Lord's face. However, I can see His hair, hands and clothing, and I can tell that He has a very large frame. His wavy hair is parted in the middle, is curled in at the bottom, comes down to His neck and is as white as silk. The

> skin on His hands is olive – coloured, and His fingers are long and slender.
>
> "I can see the Lord's mouth moving when He speaks to me. His stature and build make Him appear as if He is a young man, perhaps between the ages of thirty and forty. His height, it seems, is approximately six feet.
>
> "Although I can't make out His distinct facial features, I can tell when He is angry, happy, sad or concerned. I know Him to be very gentle and loving."

These visions and encounters continued for several months as Jesus showed Choo the reality of the spiritual realm and what heaven and hell were like. Her book and testimony have had some mixed reviews and caused debate regarding its content which at times does seem rather strange. Even David Yonggi Cho, who has enthusiastically promoted the book, writes the following in the foreword, "Please do not consider this a theological thesis or a book on doctrine. Just read it and enjoy it as the author's personal experience and testimony about what she has seen and heard in heaven."

Such visions and encounters do make us realise that we are not physical beings with a spirit but spiritual beings with a physical body.

26

“MOMMY – I SAW JESUS!”

After our four-year-old son nearly drowned, the doctors told us he would never be the same again. They were right!

The following account was reported in *Christianity Today International* in November 2002 and tells the fascinating story of a four-year-old's encounter with Jesus after drowning and making a full recovery. His mother tells the story,

“It began as a typical late spring evening in our little city of Tuscaloosa, Alabama, USA. But June 15, 2000, was destined to become a night my family will never forget. My oldest son Jacob's junior league baseball team had just lost a playoff game that, on paper, they were supposed to win. My husband, Craig, who was helping coach the team with a friend, had promised the boys that if they won, they would have a big pool party. But seeing the sulking faces of a bunch of 10-year-olds, Craig and his friend decided to let the boys have the party anyway.

“So, at the home of one of the young players, the team and their families enjoyed the warm evening air. Everyone was having a great time in and around the pool. After swimming, we all gathered together to eat on the patio. The nine-foot-deep pool lay 20 yards away.

“After getting our five children settled, my husband and I sat down to eat. Kennedy, our four-year-old son, sat a few feet away on his towel, eating a hot dog with the ‘big boys.’

“Halfway through my meal, I realised Kennedy was no longer on his towel. At this point, many of the younger children had finished eating and were up playing on bikes and riding toys. I thought Kennedy was probably riding one of the toys, but I had an overwhelming sense that I needed to find my son.

“I immediately went to the pool but did not see him. I scanned the area in and around the pool, looking for his little red swimsuit. I never thought to look on the bottom of the pool's deep end. I headed to the front of the house thinking the street would be the next worst place he could be.

“I returned to the patio and told Craig that I could not find Kennedy. He also got up and went to the pool area. We searched and called for more than five minutes. As we were both returning from searching around the yard we heard the screams. Above them all was our 10-year-old son, Jacob, yelling, ‘Daddy, Daddy, Kennedy was on the bottom of the pool!’ I heard someone yell, ‘Call 911!’

“I ran toward the pool, and what I saw makes my heart ache even now. There on the concrete lay my precious Kennedy. He was limp, bloated to twice his size, and his colouring was a sick, greyish blue. Craig, a family physician, was already crouched over our son, performing CPR. Kneeling behind him were two men praying and quoting Scripture.

“‘This could not be happening,’ I said to myself, ‘not to my child.’ I fell to my knees, grabbing Kennedy's legs, which felt like rubber, and prayed for the Lord to please save my son. I found out later that Kennedy did not have a heartbeat for the first five minutes of CPR.

"After twelve minutes of CPR, the ambulance arrived. Kennedy was breathing and he had a heart rate of 120. Craig rode to the hospital in the ambulance with Kennedy. Our five-week-old baby son and I were driven by our dear friend, who was also one of the men on their knees praying for Kennedy. This friend prayed and quoted Scripture the entire trip.

"After arriving at the local hospital, Kennedy was intubated. His lungs were swelling and he was having seizures and posturing, which is a sign of brain damage.

"Several of Craig's medical colleagues were there at the hospital, taking care of Kennedy. They worked feverishly, but they were not optimistic about his chances. He had been without oxygen for too long. The pediatrician who had trained Craig several years before actually pulled me aside and explained how bleak the situation was, that Kennedy would likely have severe brain damage – if, in fact, he survived.

"The ER doctors worked diligently, but they knew Kennedy needed to get to the children's hospital in Birmingham for the best care. It was a 20-minute trip for Kennedy on the *Lifesaver* helicopter. It would take Craig and I an hour by car. As we left, we knew things were not looking good for our little boy."

A Small Comfort

"When we arrived at Children's Hospital, we were amazed at everyone who drove to Birmingham to support and pray for us. The prayers began to ripple through our community. After the doctors worked on Kennedy, the ICU physician came out to tell us that Kennedy was in a critical condition but there was a chance for survival. He told us Kennedy might not recognize us and that he might thrash around uncontrollably. He also told us that there was a five day waiting period during which Kennedy's brain could begin swelling.

"After the doctor left, I again prayed for my precious little boy. I prayed for complete healing, but I would take Kennedy anyway God would give him back to me.

"We were able to see Kennedy a few hours later. My little man had tubes everywhere, one down his throat into his lungs, one arterial line into his heart, numerous ivs, and a catheter in his bladder. He was a pitiful sight, but he was alive."

Out of The Deep Waters

"The next few days consisted of waiting and praying. Kennedy's lungs were very sick. Yet, two days after being found and pulled off the bottom of a swimming pool by a team of nine and ten-year-old boys (a miracle in itself), our little son began to show signs that he was still with us.

"The first signs were fighting with the tube down his throat, squeezing our hands on command, and the most exciting moment was the first time he gave us a little thumbs up. Throughout this time of waiting God sent us caring family, friends, and hospital staff. But most comforting was His Word. Each day the Lord spoke to us through Scripture.

"On Sunday, June 18, God told me to read Psalm 18,

> *"He reached down from on high and took hold of me; he drew me out of deep waters. He rescued me from my powerful enemy, from my foes, who were too strong for me. They confronted me in the day of my disaster, but the Lord was my support. He brought me out into a spacious place; he rescued me because he delighted in me,"* (vv. 16-19, NIV).

"I knew my little boy was going to be completely healed.

"Exactly one week after the accident Kennedy was released from Children's Hospital. A child who was supposed to die, or at least have severe brain damage, left the hospital on his granddad's shoulders. Minutes after arriving back home in Tuscaloosa, he asked his dad, 'Daddy, will you play baseball with me?' I am sure you can guess what his daddy's answer was."

To Heaven and Back

"The story of Kennedy's accident and healing is a miracle by itself. But there is so much more.

"I desperately wanted to know how Kennedy got on the bottom of that pool. There were almost 40 people at the party, and no one saw him get in the pool. Why hadn't I watched him more closely? The guilt began to gnaw away at my conscience.

"After Kennedy was able to talk, I said, 'You were asleep for a long time, I have been missing you. What did you do?' He answered, 'An angel picked me up and we flew. We flew through walls, clouds, and I flew through you, Mommy.'

"I asked him what the angel looked like, and he told me the angel had long, white clothes. Kennedy told me they flew to heaven and that there was a door with jewels all around it and 'When they opened that door, it was snowing in there.'

"I was careful not to put words in Kennedy's mouth, I wanted this to be his memory. The only time I asked him a detailed question was when I asked him if he had seen his Uncle Mark in heaven (who had died of brain cancer six months earlier). Kennedy told me

that he did see Mark in heaven and that he looked 'just like Jesus.' He told me Mark was happy and that he wanted to stay in heaven.

"Kennedy told me that Jesus held him and that there were a lot of angels. Kennedy also described seeing a volcano. He told me, 'There were people in the volcano, there was a dragon in there with them and they were sad, there was fire all around the volcano.'

"As Kennedy was describing all this to me I asked him continually if he was ever afraid. He said, 'No, I was with Jesus and Uncle Mark, and I was standing on glass; I was invisible.' I asked Kennedy how he got back, and he told me Uncle Mark gave him a push and an angel flew him back. I asked him if he would like to go back to heaven again someday, and he said, 'Yes, but Jesus is coming here.'

"Kennedy was a little boy who two weeks before his accident would have gotten upset if you discussed death and going to heaven with him. He was just four, and he wasn't prepared for that. He didn't want to leave Mommy. Now, suddenly, he's a boy who tells us about Jesus and heaven with excitement and joy. Our son saw Jesus.

"Many people have asked us how this experience has changed our lives. For one thing, it has turned us into fanatics when it comes to children and swimming safety. But more important, it has given our family a boldness to shout from the mountaintops what the Lord did for our little boy and what awaits us when we leave this world.

"I know that Kennedy's experience will sound unbelievable to most people. And I understand. In fact, it would mean nothing to us if we did not have God's Word. Kennedy's story is a whisper, and God's Word is the trumpet."

27

JESUS IN THE MIDST

In the state *Three Self Church* of China the Communist authorities fiercely discourage all forms of evangelism. All outreach to children is strictly forbidden and certain parts of the Bible cannot be preached, such as the Second Coming of Jesus. The government will not allow the state churches to teach divine healing or deliverance from demons and the entire book of Revelation is banned.

The story of the Christian church in China oppressed under Communism is inspiring. Communist regimes such as China always regard Christianity as a threat to their very existence, because of their atheistic political ideology. During the dark years of Chairman Mao's "Great Leap Forward" (launched in 1958) and "The Great Proletarian Cultural Revolution" (1966), multitudes of Christian leaders were killed and imprisoned for their faith, and many others spent years in hard labour camps. The Communists thought they were destroying the church, but little did they realise how Jesus was watching over and walking in the midst of His church.

Led primarily by elderly women who had escaped the Communist purges, small house churches sprouted all over the country. Their very existence was and still is illegal. Fifty years of oppression and persecution has seen this church grow from around one million believers in 1949 to as many as 200 million today and growing at a rate of more than 35,000 a day or more than 12 million a year.

The presence of Jesus changes everything. It turns a filthy cell into a heavenly sanctuary. This was the experience the Apostle John had on the Isle of Patmos where he had been imprisoned for his faith.

Tradition tells us all the other apostles were dead having died martyrs' deaths, only John was now alive. Jesus had indicated in John 21 that this would be the case and church tradition tells us that the Emperor Domitian had tried to execute John by boiling him in oil but miraculously his life was preserved and he was then banished to the salt mines of Patmos. This Apostle's work was not yet finished and now as an old man of about 90 years of age, chained in his prison cell he experiences a revelation of Jesus greater than anything he had ever known before.

At this time the Emperor was claiming to be a god and venting his maniacal, demonic fury against the church. Some Christians had lost their lives, many more their homes and possessions. They had thought Jesus was coming soon but instead they and their loved ones were being persecuted and killed. John was aware of what was happening on the mainland and as he prayed and worshipped he was in the spirit.

The Lord's Day

Sunday is always called "the first day of the week" in Scripture and there is no reference to it being called "the Lord's Day" in the Early Church. John is here speaking about a special day throughout the Roman Empire known as the "Lordy Day," (the literal Greek translates it as the Imperial Day). It was the day on which emperor worship reached its climax.

Emperor worship was the one religion which covered the whole Empire and it was because of their refusal to conform to its demands that Christians were persecuted and killed. Its essence was that the reigning Roman emperor, as embodying the spirit of Rome, was divine. Once a year everyone in the Empire had to appear before a magistrate to burn a pinch of incense to the godhood of Caesar and say "Caesar is lord." Once they had done this they could go and worship any god or goddess they wished. To refuse to do this was considered not just an act of irreligion but an act of political disloyalty and rebellion. Jews were excused this because of their obvious refusal to worship any idol or graven image but Christians were not. The early Christians weren't just persecuted for worshipping Jesus but because they refused to worship anyone else.

Jesus is in Control

The book of Revelation is an Apocalyptic book, an unfolding of 1:19 *"What is now and what is to come."* Literally the word means "to see behind the veil," as to what is taking place in heaven and the purposes of God as they will be outworked.

Domitian may be on the throne in Rome, over the world's mightiest empire, but God is on the throne in heaven whose rule extends over all, and it is He not an earthly ruler that is in sovereign control. The main theme of the book of Revelation is "Jesus is King," He is in complete control. The emperor may claim to have the power of life and death with the twist of his thumb but Jesus is the living one, *"who was dead and now behold is alive for ever and ever and holds the keys of death and Hades,"* (Revelation 1:18). *"He is the ruler of the Kings of the Earth,"* (Revelation 1:5).

To be an emperor is to be a '"King of Kings," but it is not Domitian in Rome, but Jesus in heaven and in the midst of His church who is the true *"King of kings and Lord of lords,"* (Revelation 17:14, 19:16).

The Description of Jesus

I always come to this vision with a feeling of total inadequacy to expound and explain what John saw. This is an encounter that needs to be read and heard and then experienced by the power of the Holy Spirit.

Jesus walks among the candlesticks in the midst of His church. He knows everything that they are doing and experiencing. He is not like a president of the company who sits in an ivory office and has no real idea of what's taking place on the shop floor. To every church He says, *"I know."*

John had seen Jesus many times. He saw Him change water into wine, (John 2:11). He saw Him raise Lazarus from the dead and reveal His glory (John 11:4, 40). He had seen His awesome splendour on the Mount of Transfiguration but he had never seen Him like this. Even though he was in the spirit he falls at Jesus' feet as though dead. Jesus has to assure John that even though His appearance has changed He is still the same. He places His right hand on him and says, *"Do not be afraid. I am the First and the Last. I am the Living One; I was dead, and behold I am alive for ever and ever! And I hold the keys of death and Hades,"* (Revelation 1:18).

He was now glorified again with the glory He had with the Father before the world begun, John 17:5.

John says everything about Him is majestic. Jesus looked both human and divine. Not stripped naked hanging on a cross but dressed in long, priestly and kingly robes with hair as white as wool, His face shining like the sun in all its brilliance.

> *"Among the lampstands was someone "like a son of man," dressed in a robe reaching down to his feet and with a golden sash around his chest. His head and hair were white like wool, as white as snow, and his eyes were like blazing fire. His feet were like bronze glowing in a furnace, and his voice was like the sound of rushing waters. In his right hand he held seven stars, and out of his mouth came a sharp double- edged sword. His face was like the sun shining in all its brilliance.*
>
> *When I saw him, I fell at his feet as though dead. Then he placed his right hand on me and said: "Do not be afraid. I am the First and the Last. I am the Living One; I was dead, and behold I am alive for ever and ever! And I hold the keys of death and Hades,* Revelation 1:13-18.

On the next page is a photograph taken from an aeroplane during an electrical storm by a Christian travelling from Australia to New Zealand in 1980. The full story was printed in a UK Christian magazine in 1984. [1]

As a result of this picture and the story behind it the person who developed the film and his whole family became believers.

I pray that the encounters with Jesus you have read of in this book will cause your faith to rise in God and that you will put your trust in Jesus, so that one day you too will see Him face to face as your Lord and Saviour.

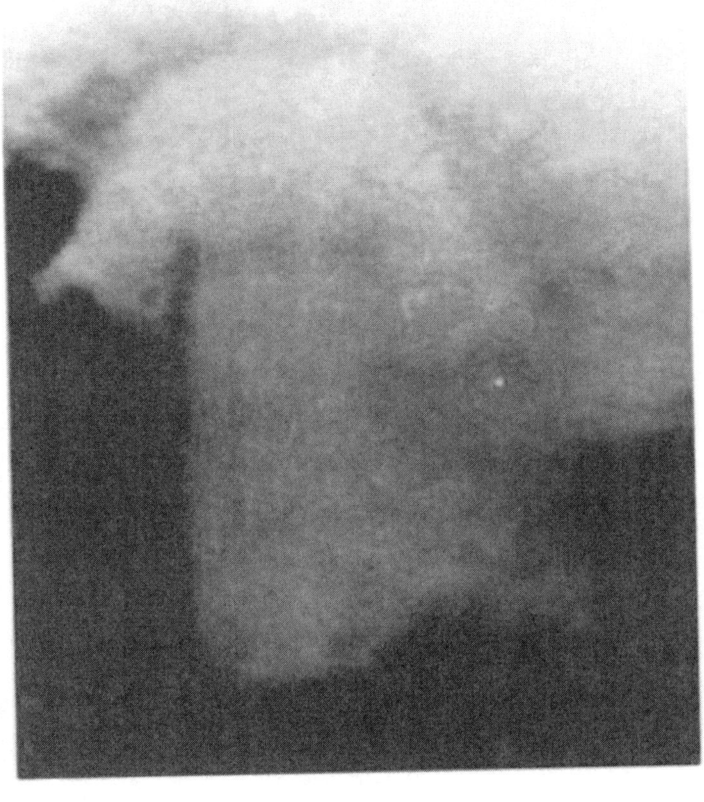

APPENDIX 1

DISCERNMENT

In 1976 the British astronomer Patrick Moore announced on BBC Radio 2 that at 9:47am, a once-in-a-lifetime astronomical event was going to occur that listeners could experience in their very own homes. The planet Pluto would pass behind Jupiter, temporarily causing a gravitational alignment that would counteract and lessen the Earth's own gravity. Moore told his listeners that if they jumped in the air at the exact moment that this planetary alignment occurred, they would experience a strange floating sensation. When 9:47am arrived, the BBC began to receive hundreds of phone calls from listeners claiming to have felt the sensation. One woman even reported that she and her eleven friends had risen from their chairs and floated around the room. Moore's announcement had been an April Fool's Day joke.

There is no doubt that some people's capacity to be gullible is enormous while others' tendency to be critical and dismissive is equally colossal. The Greek word for discernment – *diakrino* – simply means "to make a judgment or a distinction." Discernment has one primary function: to distinguish right from wrong. Discernment in Scripture is the skill that enables us to differentiate. It is the ability to see issues clearly.

Paul's counsel, *"Do not put out the Spirit's fire; do not treat prophecies with contempt. Test everything. Hold on to the good. Avoid every kind of evil,"* 1Thessalonians 5:19-22, is very important because we are naturally conditioned to have a prejudice for the negative. In other words, we are more likely to examine something for the purpose of proving that it is false rather than confirming that it is true.

It often happens when people think they are exercising discernment when in reality they are really being judgmental. They mistake spiritual perception for what is personal preference and prejudice fuelled by preconceived ideas. The danger with this is that we can all be guilty. Let those without sin cast the first stone. What's more frightening is that most times we aren't aware we are doing it. In other words, we have failed to discern the truth about ourselves, never mind that which we are supposed to be evaluating. So how do we test everything? It's a Scripture quoted equally passionately by those on both sides of theological debate who think by articulating its requirement it brings weight to their argument. But there is a world, or better still, a kingdom of difference between acknowledging a truth and being able to apply it.

Foundation - Focus - Fruit

God's Word must be our foundation and Jesus our focus.

Then there is another test, one that Jesus referred to when He warned about false prophets, that is to test the fruit of what is being said and done, Matthew 7.

So foundation, focus and fruit are three key words in seeking to evaluate even the most complex issues. They also help us to evaluate the accounts of appearances of Jesus that we have read in this book.

The writer and teacher A W Tozer said in his book *The Divine Conquest*, that the greatest gift we need in the church is the gift of discernment and added, “I would bring everything to the test of the Word and the Spirit. Not the Word only, but the Word and the Spirit. *‘God is Spirit,’* said our Lord, *‘and they that worship Him must worship in Spirit and in truth.’* While it is never possible to have the Spirit without at least some measure of truth, it is unfortunately, possible to have a shell of truth without the Spirit. Our hope is that we may have both the Spirit and the truth in fuller measure.”

When the Sadducees tried to trick Jesus by questioning Him about the resurrection, He answered them by saying they were in error because they did not know the Scriptures or the power of God. It is interesting to note that you can fall into error by not only being ignorant in your knowledge of the Word but by also being limited in your understanding of God's power. The Sadducees didn't believe in miracles, angels, the supernatural or the resurrection of the dead so Jesus rightly chides them for their unbelief. They had decided what God could and could not do but Jesus says God is not boxed into their system.

Dennis Hensley writes about the training procedures that American Air Force pilots have to go through, “One flight condition a pilot must understand is hypoxia or ‘oxygen starvation.’ Students are paired off in an altitude simulation chamber. With oxygen masks on, they are taken to simulated conditions of 30,000 feet. Then one student in each pair removes his mask for a few minutes and begins to answer simple questions on a sheet of paper. Suddenly, their partners force the oxygen masks on the uncovered mouths and noses of the people who are writing. After a few gulps of normal air, each writer is astounded at what he sees on his paper. The first few written lines are legible, but the last few lines are unreadable. One minute earlier, the participant was absolutely sure he had written his answers in perfectly legible script. In reality, he was on the verge of losing total consciousness."

Likewise without the Holy Spirit, the breath of God, our ability to perceive truth and reality becomes distorted.

In the testimonies in this book I have used the above principles of *foundation – focus – fruit*. I have sought at all times to evaluate such experiences in the light of God's Word and whether or not they are consistent with what we know of Jesus and that they bring glory to Him. The *fruit* of such encounters is also of great importance as in each case mentioned there are tangible results of God's love and power.

When the Word of God is our foundation and Jesus is our focus the Holy Spirit will lead us into a deeper knowledge and experience with Jesus who is the truth.

"I keep asking that the God of our Lord Jesus Christ, the glorious Father, may give you the Spirit of wisdom and revelation, so that you may know him better," Ephesians 1:17.

APPENDIX 2

VISIONS and DREAMS

Islamic Faithful "See Jesus" After Ramadan

Christian Broadcasting Network reported the following amazing story from Zamboanga City in the Philippines, "A number of Muslim faithfuls here could hardly believe what they saw in their dreams weeks after Ramadan, a 30-day period of prayer and fasting by followers of the Islam Faith."

The details were given by Mohaimin Datu, a Christian Evangelical missionary to the Tausugs, the largest Muslim tribe in the Philippines. Datu is also the regional coordinator of the Tausug ministry, a project of the Philippine Mission's Association for the Southern Philippines.

Datu relayed accounts of some Islamic faithfuls but for security reasons requested the reporter not to reveal the names of Muslims who "saw Jesus" in their dreams. Datu shared that a Muslim resident in Sinunuc, a remote village in this city, could hardly believe when he saw *Isah* (Jesus) in a dream and He defeated a giant dragon in a duel. The resident had the same dream again the following night. According to Datu. “From that time, the person became more interested in the teachings of Jesus.

Datu added, in another related account, “an Islamic faithful from the west coast district of this city dreamt of Jesus healing many people. The following day, he shared his dream with his fellow Muslims that *Isah* (Jesus) can heal sickness. The Muslim faithful prayed and asked Jesus to heal those who requested prayer and they eventually experienced complete healing.”

Datu recalled that the first time he heard such similar accounts was two years previously after Ramadan when he encountered a *Yakan* (Muslim tribe) resident in Basilan Province (neighbouring island of this city) who dreamed of “The Prophet Mohammed who could not stare directly at the eyes of Jesus Christ.”

The *Yakan* dreamer was confused by what he saw in his dream, so he asked his cousin, a newly converted Christian, the meaning of that dream. His cousin replied that, “Your dream depicts that Jesus is greater than Mohammed.”

A number of Muslims continue to see visions in the city and it has been the talk of the village in the west coast, according to Datu.

Datu noted one common practice among Islamic faithfuls who dreamed about Jesus. He recounted that during Ramadan the Islamic faithfuls are required to pray five times a day to Allah (God) but they have the option to pray six to seven times a day. Datu said that these Muslim dreamers in their sixth and seventh prayer, have been asking God to reveal Himself in any form of vision and let truth reign in their lives.

"Visions of Jesus Stir Muslim Hearts"

"Throughout the nearly 1,400 year history of Islam, Muslims have resisted the Christian Gospel. But according to many reports from the Middle East and around the world, that history is changing.

"I see many, many Arabic-speaking people turning to Christ, accepting Him as Lord and Saviour," said Nizar Shaheen, host of *Light for the Nations*, a Christian programme seen throughout the Muslim world. "It's happening all over the Arab world. It's happening in North Africa. It's happening in the Middle East. It's happening in the Gulf countries. It's happening in Europe and Canada and the United States in the Arabic-speaking world. Everywhere, people are accepting Jesus."

"What's happening nowadays in the Muslim world has never happened before," said Father Zakaria Henein, an Egyptian Coptic priest who is one of the foremost evangelists to the Muslim world. He says a cross-section of Muslims are accepting Jesus Christ. "Young and old, educated and not educated, males and females – even those who are fanatic."

Heidi Baker of *Iris Ministries* sees thousands of African Muslims receiving Jesus and getting baptized. She said, "It's probably the only place in the world where they are coming so quickly, many people are having dreams and they see Jesus appear to them. Probably half our pastors were leaders, imams in Muslim mosques, now they're pastors."

"Dreams of Jesus lead Muslims to Christ in Ethiopia"

Inspire magazine carried the above headline as it told of those who were having supernatural encounters with God. Robel, an Islamic leader in Ethiopia, described how he found faith in

Christ after Jesus appeared to him in a dream. Robel was expelled from the mosque he helped to lead in 2003 for asking questions about Jesus. That same night he had a dream in which Christ appeared to him. The following morning he committed his life to the Lord and started attending church. He says, “After my conversion my house and all my property were burned, several times Muslims came to my house with a spear threatening us, trying to hurt someone.”

To try to entice Robel back, Islamists offered him the opportunity to go to Saudi Arabia for Islamic training and to return to Ethiopia a wealthy man. But he refused, preferring poverty and to sleep in trees – with the freedom to choose his own faith. “People always seek the money and the wealth of the earth, but what I seek is from God,” he told *The Voice of the Martyrs* organisation.

“Ishmael”, the son of an Islamic leader, also became a Christian after Jesus spoke to him in a dream. He was later healed of malaria when he was prayed for by a Christian evangelist. Ishmael’s father was responsible for six mosques in the area. “I was chased out of my home and was unable to go to school because a government official used to wait for me on the street everyday and intimidate me with his gun. So I stopped my education fearing that I would be killed if I was found on the streets.”

Christine Darg of *Exploits Ministry* says,

“When I share the Gospel, I usually start by asking Muslims if they have ever experienced a dream about Jesus. It is almost inevitable that they have seen Jesus and this makes proclaiming the Gospel that much easier. God’s methods of communicating with us have not changed. Today His main method of communication is through His written Word, the Bible. But the Lord still speaks to us in pictures – in dreams and visions – just as He communicated in the Bible to all ranks of people."

Darg goes on to say, "But why does the risen Lord appear differently to different people? In visions, we do not see the transfigured Lord in all of His glory, as this would be too awesome. But He chooses according to His infinite wisdom to reveal Himself in different ways or in varying cultural aspects so that people can understand, or relate to Him, and receive Him."

An article published in *Mission Frontiers* magazine reported that over one quarter of those surveyed stated quite emphatically that dreams and visions were instrumental in drawing them to Christ and sustained them through difficult times.

The survey was based on questionnaires completed by more than 600 Muslims who had placed their faith in Jesus.

A typical "Jesus dream or vision" is usually described by Muslims as a peaceful face that they somehow recognize as Jesus. Often they encounter a compassionate figure in a white robe, calling them to come to Him. Sometimes His hands and arms are extended wide, or Jesus reaches toward them in love and invitation.

APPENDIX 3

BETTY BAXTER

Original Newspaper Story
Fairmont Daily Sentinel

Miracles of healing generally seem to occur in far off places, but now it appears that one has taken place right in Martin County – in the presence of witnesses – and a girl who was hopelessly crippled two weeks ago suddenly – yes, instantly – was made well and normal and is able to walk and do the things she has not been able to do for four years. That girl is Betty Baxter, 15-year-old daughter of Mr and Mrs William Baxter of Center Creek Township.

In four years she had not been well enough to go to school, having quit in the fifth grade with what then was diagnosed as a kidney ailment. Two years ago she was taken to University Hospital and was sent home with the information that the hospital could do nothing for a serious back condition that was not fully explained to the family. Last November she collapsed during the Armistice storm and since then has grown steadily worse, until the past month or so when her back was doubled so that her head nearly touched her knees and hard lumps grew on her spine.

Then, on Sunday, August 24, at 3.10pm, in the presence of Center Creek and Nashville township neighbours and some other relatives, most of whom were kneeling and praying for her recovery, she straightened up in her chair, stood erect and walked.

Betty told two *Sentinel* reporters yesterday afternoon that she earlier had a vision of the exact time and place when her miraculous cure would take place and that she had asked her mother to invite certain neighbours to be present at the time, accounting for the fact there were so many witnesses on hand.

Betty, a sweet and frail-looking girl, said she had "word from the Lord" many times regarding her illness and ultimate recovery, but none quite so clear as the vision she had received about noon August 14 when the details of her recovery and the exact time and place were revealed to her.

She told how once in her sleep she had a communication from God, in which He asked her if she had faith that she would be healed. "I told Him, 'Sure I do'." Betty went on, "But I did not know when it would be exactly. I knew it would not be then, but in the Fall (autumn)." The August 14 vision of the time and place came to her when she suddenly lapsed into a coma while sitting in a doubled-up position in a large chair near the dining room table where the family was at dinner. She seemed to swoon away, her mother said.

Mother has a "word"

Mrs Baxter said, she, too, had the "assurance from God" that her daughter would be healed, with a particularly strong message shortly before Betty's strange vision. "The Lord has spoken to me many times," Mrs Baxter said sincerely.

The mother calmly verified Betty's statements regarding her previous and present conditions, supplied the names of the persons present, told of the details of the miraculous cure as the devout neighbours knelt in the Baxter living room and prayed for her girl, who sat hunched in an over-stuffed chair.

The entire interview was conducted in the presence of the girl's pastor, Rev Dexter Collins of the Granada Gospel Tabernacle, whom *The Sentinel* reporters had invited to accompany them to the Baxter home. Rev Collins had just returned from Chicago, where he had been preaching. Rev Collins left Granada a day or so before the girl's sudden cure and was notified of it by telegram in Chicago. He had visited the family on Friday, August 22, and had seen the girl hobble out of her bedroom, bent double head almost to her knees, and sit thus in a chair. Betty told Rev Collins at this time that he should be present Sunday at 2.30pm for she would be healed at that time. Rev Collins said he was sorry that his engagement in Chicago was taking him away, but asked that the family wire him if the cure was effected. This the family did about 4pm, or about an hour after it occurred.

Buy her new clothes

After Betty's August 14 vision, and her mother's communication from God, the family was so confident that it would occur that they went to Fairmont and bought Betty a new dress, shoes and coat. Like any normal girl, Betty asked for time yesterday afternoon to put on her new dress and shoes before she posed for any more pictures.

The first photograph of her was taken in her hose dress, hair net on her head, sitting on the arm of the chair in which she was healed, just as the reporters and Rev Collins had met her upon entering the farm house. She was startled by the flash bulb, as were her mother and little brothers and sisters grouped around her for the first photograph, then flushed prettily, probably thinking of her new dress like any normal girl would do.

The Baxter's really are not newcomers in the nearby community, although they came to the present place, the farm of Wm. M. Potter of Blue Earth, in section 6, Center Creek, the extreme northwest corner of the township, two years ago from Northfield.

Mrs Baxter was the daughter of Mr and Mrs Frank Louks of near Guckeen and Pilot Grove neighbourhoods in Fairbault County until nine years ago when they moved to Northfield where they lived two years before coming back to Martin County. The Frank Louks now live at Owatonna. Betty was born on a farm near Guckeen. There are seven children in the Baxter family, namely: Dorothy, 20; Wanda, 17; Betty, 15; Evelyn, 13; Billy, 12; Kenneth, 6 and Ross, 4. Yesterday, Dorothy was at the home of her aunt, Mrs Earl Adams, near Imogene, and Wanda was helping out at the George Sturm home. It was while at Northfield that Betty became ill with what Mrs Baxter said was a kidney ailment and she was not well for the next two years, having to quit school.

While still at Northfield, Betty was taken to *University Hospital* for treatments and remained there for about two weeks. Many X-rays were taken of Betty's spine and the young girl said the doctors there then told her there was nothing they could do for her, that her spine was in very bad shape, and that she should to quote Betty's own words, "Go home and enjoy life as long as possible." Betty volunteered, "But I knew God would heal me."

All this time, up to last November, Betty could not do housework, or any of the things young girls normally do. She could push a chair around the floor, but could not lift it. She became gradually weaker, had frequent attacks and severe backaches from time to time. Then came the incident of the Armistice Day storm last November. "Daddy told me to come to the door and look out at the wind and the snow," Betty said. "I went to the door and then I fell down." Mrs Baxter said the girl did not fall so as to injure herself, but simply crumpled to the floor and that she caught Betty as she was falling.

Toward the last, her mother provided her with an open front housecoat, it being impossible to put on a dress in her crippled condition. Rev Collins saw her on his visit the Friday before her cure. "I knew the family was terribly depressed," Rev Collins said, "so I made it a point to visit them just before I left and see if I could encourage them. I saw Betty all doubled up and I knew that if something did not change soon, that she could not live long. Then she told me about her strange vision and asked me to be present Sunday as a witness."

In recent weeks strange lumps apparently as hard as bone, had appeared on Betty's spine, beginning near the base of her neck and continuing downward. Rev Collins said he saw the lumps and touched the one on her neck when he visited there a week ago Friday. Mrs Baxter, the children, and neighbours had seen them, too, and said they were about half as large as a hen's egg.

Tells of Vision

Betty was asked to tell more about her visions and talks with her God and asked if she could hear the words as if they were spoken out loud. Betty and her mother said the words were not heard as if spoken by a human being, but that they heard them in their minds, or spirit, most distinctly and knew exactly what was meant each time. Betty said she had a vision of heaven with the angels all around waiting anxiously for God to appear and that she saw Jesus approaching. "There was a little tree, all bent double, and God touched the tree and it straightened up at once," said Betty. "Then I knew that would be me, and I also knew at the same time it would be on Sunday afternoon about 2.30pm."

Neighbours Called

At Betty's request, her mother called the nearby neighbours, Mr and Mrs George Sturm, John Sturm, Mrs George Teubner and Mr and Mrs Earl Adams, the latter sister of Mrs Baxter. The neighbours began to assemble shortly before 2.30pm, but John Sturm had company at home and could not come. Present were Mrs George Teubner and her mother, Mrs Strosser of Missouri; Mr and Mrs George Sturm, near neighbors; Mr and Mrs Earl Adams and two children, Donald, 19, and Viola, 17, and Donald's wife, living near the Imogene corner; and Lawrence Louks of Owatonna, a brother of Mrs Baxter, who had happened to call that day, and all nine of the Baxter family.

Betty said she previously had had the "word" regarding whom to call for the occasion, thus accounting for the numerous persons present. At about 2.30pm, most of the group began to pray for Betty's recovery, kneeling in the small living room near Betty's chair where she was hunched. Mrs Earl Adams had her hand on Betty's bent back when the miracle occurred at 3.10pm.

Back Straightens Up

Mrs Adams said she could feel Betty's back straightening steadily and in a few moments it was perfectly normal, and the mysterious lumps had disappeared. All of those present testified to hearing cracking noises as though bones were snapping back into place. Betty's older sister, Wanda, 17, said the noises were like when the Winnebago osteopath gave her treatments a number of months before. All of a sudden, Betty was sitting erect, and then she stood up and stepped over to a nearby dining room chair and lifted it off the floor. "See what the God I serve can do!" She cried.

The assembled group, of course, was astounded, but made no unusual display, letting the girl obey her natural impulses, the first of which was to go to the neighbour John Sturm, who was unable to be present, and show him what had happened.

Neighbour is Astounded

Mrs Baxter complied with Betty's request immediately and took her in the family car to the John Sturm place, only a very short distance down the road. Betty said she walked into the Sturm home and that Mr Sturm was astounded to see her walking erect and looking happily at him. "Am I dreaming?" Betty said Mr Sturm asked her. Then Betty said Mr Sturm asked her if she was going to church. "Nothing can keep me home," Betty said she told him. It is a fact that Betty, that same evening, went to the Gospel Tabernacle church service in Granada with her parents and others and there testified as to her cure. She had not been able to go to church for more than a year.

The next Sunday, September 1, she again went to church and sang with the choir morning and evening and again testified as to her recovery. She was the happiest girl in the world and everyone said she sang beautifully.

Normal at Home

At home, since her cure, Betty for the first time in four years has had no pains or aches of any kind. She walks around the house and yard normally and her mother said she even had taken a walk down to nearby Elm Creek. Evidence of her alacrity was displayed yesterday afternoon when she was asked to come outdoors for another picture, which she did, and then ran back into the house to put on her new dress. She walked about the yard with her family and visitors and then went to sit on the porch railing. Suddenly, she jumped down, went in the house, and came out with her coat on. It was rather chilly about 6pm. "Is that your new coat that you got before it happened?" a reporter asked her. "Yes," she smiled happily and girlishly. She seemed to have forgotten those weeks when her mother had to help her into the housecoat, being unable to get into a regular dress.

Mr Sturm Verifies

Upon leaving the Baxter place, the reporters and Rev Collins went to the George Sturm home to interview one of the witnesses. Mrs Sturm was busy cooking supper, and Wanda Baxter, Betty's older sister, was helping cook good old fried potatoes and pork and salad and tomatoes and cake, etc., for silo fillers who were just coming in to eat, but she took time off to talk for a few minutes.

Mrs Sturm told of Betty's hunched condition and of having seen her often in the two years the family lived as neighbours. She said she was kneeling, not looking at Betty, when the moment of the cure occurred, but that in an instant she saw her sitting straight up, then get up and lift the chair. Her story was essentially the same as that told by Betty and her mother.

Father is Happy

Just as the visitors were about to leave, William Baxter, Betty's father, came around the barn and was introduced by Rev Collins. He was all smiles and seemed to be the happiest man in the world, even if he was a bit bashful about the dust and grease from running a corn cutter. "You know, we can see and hear enough to believe these things," he said, "but this certainly proves to all of us that there is a higher power taking care of us." Baxter was a bit hesitant about having his photograph taken in his work clothes, but finally consented to have a picture with his daughter, Wanda, who came out of the house in her kitchen apron, flushed and as happy as her father. The Baxters all seem to be sturdy every -day folk and certainly Betty is no longer a care as she had been for her mother in recent months.

Neighbourhood is Happy

Everyone in the neighbourhood is extremely happy over the strange occurrence. Many stories have begun to go around concerning the case, some of which were becoming exaggerated and erroneous through constant repetition. Betty has promised to take good care of herself and both scientific and church people are anxious to watch her case. There is no doubt in Betty's mind or in the mind of her family, that she is permanently cured, and of course, everyone hopes so.

It is truly the strangest case *The Sentinel* men ever had to cover and the interview could have lasted for hours. As recently as last month, Betty Baxter was examined by a Fairmont physician. With Betty 's consent, and the consent of her mother, the newsmen interviewed the physician. "I would not say such a miracle as you have related is impossible," he said. "In fact it is wholly probable. I advised she go to Rochester for examination. I am glad to hear of her healing, and hope that her good condition will continue." Today was a happy day for Betty and her family. They set out for Owatonna to see her grandparents, Mr and Mrs Frank Louks, planning to stay at least until Friday. It was her first vacation in a long, long time.

Only one picture of the Baxter girl was taken during her crippled condition, this on the day of her cure, but the photograph was not immediately available, having been sent away to be developed. The Baxter family will give the picture to *The Sentinel* as soon as it returns, along with another picture taken immediately after she became well.

Betty has been a highly religious girl, active in Sunday school work and choir singing in which she particularly delighted. Hanging in the Baxter living room is a picture of Christ, which Mrs Baxter said was Betty's favourite picture. Betty would sit in the over-stuffed chair and contemplate the picture for long periods. Another plaque in the room says, "God is the Head of this Household."

The Sentinel has attempted to present the entire case in an entirely dispassionate manner, with facts from personal interviews only from persons who knew the Baxter girl. One motive was to still wild rumours and inaccurate tales already started about the strange case. The story is one of the strangest and most gripping that has occurred in the annals of this newspaper. The incident certainly has done much to strengthen the faith of the people in Betty's community.

For Verification of the Authenticity of this News Story, Contact:

The Sentinel
64 Downtown Plaza
P.O. Box 681
Fairmont, MN 56031

You can hear Betty's testimony on the internet at
http://www.geocities.com/bettybaxterstory/index2.html

APPENDIX 4

VISIONS AND ENCOUNTERS WITH CHRIST

A Brief Summary of Church History

Appearances and visions of Jesus Christ mark Christianity from its beginning. One of the greatest statements ever made is, *"The Word became flesh and dwelt among us,"* John 1:14.

God in Christ did not become a man for just 33 years; Jesus' incarnation and resurrection eternalized His humanity forever. Even though His body was supernaturally different after He rose from the grave it was nevertheless still a body of flesh and bones (Luke 24:39).

Jesus' post resurrection appearances provided the evidence for the extraordinary claim that Jesus was raised to live an indestructible life.

As early as the fourth century, Christian leaders offered advice to visionaries to assist them in determining whether their experiences were divine or diabolical. Athanathius, bishop of Alexandria (293-373), suggested that an apparition should be asked who it is and where it came from, adding, "And if it should be a vision of holy ones they will assure you, and change your fear into joy. But if the vision should be from the devil, immediately it becomes feeble."

He also noted that demons greatly feared the sign of the cross and were given to making worldly displays, threatening death, and "capering and changing their forms of appearances." [1]

Saint Gregory, writing at the turn of the seventh century, said that because many sources of revelation exist, we should not put faith in them. But he thought that saints could distinguish true revelations from the voices and images of illusion through an inner sensitivity. [2]

Martin Luther, the leader of the Reformation said, "I do not detract from the gifts of others, if God by chance reveals something to someone beyond Scripture through dreams, through visions, and through angels."

Luther does speak about having concluded a pact with the Lord that He should not send him any visions, dreams or angels because he had already been influenced "by that infinite multitude of illusions, deceptions, and impostures by which the world was horribly deceived for a long time through satan under the papacy." [3]

John Calvin, another great church reformer, viewed visions with suspicion,

"Satan often makes use of apparitions to make fools out of those who do not believe. The result is that the bare vision leaves a man's mind in a state of suspense. But the Spirit seals those which truly come from God with a sure mark, so that those whom God wishes to have truly devoted to Himself may not waiver or hesitate. The Lord Himself does not appear by visions."

But he does not rule out the possibility that angels might visit us and confirm the truth. [4]

Appendix 4 – Visions and Encounters with Christ
A Brief Summary of Church History

No comprehensive collection of reported Christic visions and encounters exists but Phillip Wiebe in his book *Visions of Jesus* quotes extensively from those reports which are available. Below are just a few.

1. St Porphory (353-420) while in extreme pain said he experienced a trance in which he saw Jesus upon the cross along with the penitent thief. [5]

2. St Gregory (540-604) claimed that one night as he fed the poor, Jesus appeared to him.

3. St Rosa of Viterbo (1235-1252) said she saw Jesus suspended on the cross. [6]

4. St Columba (1477-1501) claimed to have seen Jesus hung on the cross.

5. Julian of Norwich (1450) said she saw sixteen visions and apparitions of Jesus' sufferings. [7]

6. St Clara (1346) said she saw Jesus seated on His throne of glory surrounded by John the Baptist and the Apostles. [8]

7. St Barbara of Nicomedia claimed that Jesus appeared to her and healed her while she was in prison for her faith. [9]

8. Forty Christian soldiers imprisoned and awaiting execution for refusing to offer sacrifices to pagan deities are said to have been visited by Jesus in AD 320. [10]

9. St Francis of Assisi said he saw Jesus and was given by Him three white and three red roses of exquisite beauty, as an external ratification of the reality of the vision, it being in the midst of winter, when a rose was nowhere to be found. [11]

APPENDIX 5

EXPLAINING VISIONS OF AND ENCOUNTERS WITH JESUS

What Causes Them?

Something as remarkable as visions and physical encounters with Jesus are obviously going to create a great deal of discussion and debate as to whether they could be genuine and what may cause them.

1). Supernatural Explanations

These assert that visions and encounters with Jesus are the supernatural workings of God transcending the natural order. This is by far the best explanation that fits the facts of the accounts given in this book and they can be divided into four distinct groupings:

a) They are produced by the resurrected Christ making Himself known in time and space encounters. Although we need to clarify this by asking questions such as:

Are we saying that Jesus' resurrection body, although considered to have extraordinary powers, such as the ability to appear and disappear instantly and move through solid structures and not be confined to natural laws, is a body that does not vary in form – it always looks the same?

There are occasions in Scripture Luke 24 (Emmaus Road), John 20 (Mary Magdalene), when Jesus was not instantly recognised. These could have been for a variety of reasons such as they were not expecting to see Him, the sun or tears were in their eyes or they were supernaturally kept from doing so etc.

What are we to make of visions and encounters where Jesus is seen hanging on a cross or with bleeding wounds?

This is not what He is like now. Sometimes Jesus is seen with wounds and sometimes He is not, sometimes there is radiance surrounding Him but not always. Sometimes He appears normal height and other times much bigger. Sometimes His whole body is seen and other times only His face.

Therefore we cannot be dogmatic and say His body does not vary in form but we must be very careful how we define this. We are not saying that Jesus exists in numerous forms and different bodies but there are variations of His disclosure.

We cannot now see Jesus in all of His glory, as this would be too awesome, but He chooses according to His infinite wisdom to reveal Himself in different ways or in varying cultural aspects so that people can understand, or relate to Him, and receive Him. Jesus' resurrected body is therefore allowed to vary as are the perceptions of those who encounter Him.

b) While some consider Christic visions to be produced by the resurrected Christ, the Augustinian tradition teaches that corporeal visions (involving outer senses) are produced by angels mediating images from heaven. Augustine maintained that all manifestations of God except the Incarnation are mediated by angels. This has been called *The Angelic Mediation Theory*.

His idea that angels might be responsible for corporeal visions of Jesus has become embedded in Catholic thought, and is expressed in the *New Catholic Encyclopaedia* (1967).

The best example of this in Scripture would be,

"*The revelation of Jesus Christ, which God gave him to show his servants what must soon take place. He made it known by sending his angel to his servant John,*" Revelation 1:1.

Although this can happen it does not adequately explain those encounters where Jesus reaches out and touches the person resulting in remarkable healings and miracles. Neither does it bear the testimony of truth when Jesus clearly says that He is present.

c) A third explanation is referred to as *The Holy Spirit Theory*. This is similar to *The Angelic Mediation Theory* but with the Holy Spirit mediating the images of Jesus.

Again this is possible as long as it isn't inferred that the Holy Spirit has a physical body. While obviously the Holy Spirit is at work where there are genuine visions and encounters with Jesus the resurrection accounts in Scripture make it quite clear that the person being seen is actually Jesus. There is no reason to assume otherwise in other encounters when Jesus clearly expresses it is Himself.

d) There is, of course, a fourth possibility that the visions and encounters are demonic in nature and not of God but the devil.

I have come across a number in the course of my research for this book that I did not include that I would classify this way, but because there is a counterfeit you don't simply dismiss and deny the genuine. It is dangerous to give such power and purpose to the devil for him to deceive us and so little to God to reveal Himself to us.

There is far too much positive evidence of God at work to attribute it all to the devil. There are wonderful healings, conversions and deliverances from evil bondage that glorify Jesus.

The Bible does give us a clear command *"to test the spirits whether they are of God"* (1 John 4:1) and "*prove everything*" (1 Thessalonians 5:21). So we must always be very careful about evaluating such testimony in the light of Scripture as bearing the stamp of truth. And we must be equally careful not to merely dismiss it as the talk of a confused mind or demonic apparition.

2). Psychological and Neurophysiological Explanations

The second group of explanations comes from the psychological sciences, where the term "hallucination" is often used to refer to visions. The *Oxford English Dictionary* describes hallucination as "The apparent perception (usually by sight or hearing) of an external object when no such object is actually present." In other words, seeing or hearing things that aren't there. Of course such things can and do occur especially when there is some extreme mental or physical state (a mirage in the desert for instance) or through certain drugs and medications or substance abuse. To describe something as being "an hallucination" is usually to term it in a derogatory sense.

Recent explanations are that such things are brought on by expecting them to occur, or through stress, loneliness, depression or an intense desire to make them happen.

This class of explanations has been supplemented with ones that also use the conceptual resources of neurophysiology. The *"perceptual release theory"* is one of the most popular. It maintains that information obtained through sensory perception is stored, altered, and then "released into consciousness" at a later time and experienced as an hallucination or a dream. But there is no psychological explanation able to explain the capacity to look away from the vision, and then see it again upon looking back to the place where the vision was first seen.

Consider the stress theory as an example. According to this theory, stress supposedly causes a person to see a vision of Jesus. But when that person turns away from the figure that appeared they no longer see it, supposedly because stress had become sufficiently reduced. When they turn again to face the direction in which they first saw the vision, stress was presumably sufficiently increased so that the vision is seen again.

Of course, neurophysiological capacities are involved, but no mind or hallucinatory theory can accommodate many of the experiences (such as group encounters, remarkable healings and words of knowledge) described in these pages. Neither can illusions, which are misperceptions of actual external stimuli. Such explanations are clearly inadequate as the encounters are too clear and structured with external evidence pointing to their validity. The accounts given in this book are not of people who were suffering with fevers, intoxication, withdrawal from drugs, sensory deprivation or psychiatric disorders which are the common causes of hallucinations. They are those from a wide range of life and background who would be considered, "perfectly normal" and in many case extremely well educated.

APPENDIX 6

INTERPRETATIONS OF VISIONS AND ENCOUNTERS

Augustine in the 4th century was the first to give a sustained discussion of Christic encounters and apparitions in Christian theological history. In his book *The Literal Meaning of Genesis* he distinguishes three kinds of vision:

Corporeal: A bodily vision which uses the powers of sight. The other two kinds of vision do not.

The vast majority of visions and encounters detailed in this book belong to the first category of corporeal visions as they involved the human senses.

Imaginative: A spiritual vision which is an experience that takes place as a result of the activity of the human imagination.

Intellectual: A vision is an experience by means of which we receive understanding through an intuition and enlightening of the mind.

Martin Luther, the great Reformer, also makes a threefold distinction between kinds of revelatory experience which are different from Augustine. Luther's distinction is far more Bible based and derives from Numbers 12:6-8,

"When a prophet of the Lord is among you, I reveal myself to him in visions, I speak to him in dreams. But this is not true of my servant Moses; he is faithful in all my house. With him I speak face to face, clearly and not in riddles; he sees the form of the Lord."

Dreams:	Luther considered to be the lowest form of revelation.
Visions:	When God appears to a person while awake then it can be a form of apparition.
Face to Face:	This is the highest form of revelation and far more trustworthy. God is here speaking from a direct encounter and enlightening the heart with the rays of the Holy Spirit.

Luther said, "All revelations must be in harmony with Scripture and if they are not or destroy faith they are of satan." [1]

APPENDIX 7

SOME INTRIGUING QUESTIONS

1. *There is no physical description of Jesus given in the Bible – the closest we get is from Isaiah 53, "Nothing in his appearance that we should desire him." This is very tentative at best and so is the reference when the Pharisees said, "You are not yet 50-years-old," John 10.*

   Therefore how did those who have seen and encountered Him know immediately it was Jesus?

I believe at least part of the answer is that as well as a physical encounter there was also a spiritual revelation by the Holy Spirit who has come to lead us into all truth and glorify Jesus.

There is also the mention of radiance, glory, supernatural light and a sense of awe and wonder.

Jesus communicates in ways people can understand. For instance, He spoke in different languages to those He encountered and sometimes they had memories of His likeness from a picture or painting and Jesus appeared like this so they would know who He was.

On a number of occasions Jesus spoke saying who He was and why He had come.

2. *In some visions and encounters Jesus is seen with nail prints and wounds and in others He isn't.*

We know Jesus had such wounds after the resurrection as He told Thomas to put his hand in them and feel them, John 20, but neither the Apostles Paul or John make mention of them in their encounters. Either they did not notice them or more likely the glory was so great and they were so overwhelmed the nail prints were not their focus.

Were the nails driven through the hands or wrists?

When Jesus reached Golgotha (the hill outside the city gate of Jerusalem) He was placed on His back, arms stretched out and nailed to the cross bar. The nails were about 7-9 inches long.

The nails would normally have been placed between the bones of the forearm (the radius and ulna) and the small bones of the hands (the carpal bones). The placement of the nails at these points had several effects.

First, it ensured that the victim would hang there until dead.

Secondly, it would sever the median nerve causing intense pain. The destruction of this nerve causes permanent paralysis of the hand. Furthermore, by nailing the victim at this point in the wrist, there would be minimal bleeding and there would be no bones broken.

But is there evidence that the nails were driven through the hands?

Christian tradition often shows the nails as driven through the palms. In the Bible, the nails were said to be driven into the hands of Jesus. (Medically, the hands include the wrists.)

Recent studies of ancient crucifixions have revealed that the nails were sometimes driven through the hands as opposed to the wrists. The hands have a nerve running through the middle of them that would have caused unbelievable amounts of pain when the nail was driven through. To support the body's weight, ropes were tied at the wrists and the elbows to tie them to the crossbeam, then the legs were broken causing the weight of their body to pull on the upper body, eventually resulting in death by slow suffocation.

The Greek meaning of the word “hands” includes the wrist.

3. *When Jesus was at one location on earth did it mean that He had left heaven?*

There are several post ascension visions and encounters with Jesus mentioned in the New Testament. The most significant of these are to John on the island of Patmos and to Paul on the Damascus Road resulting in Paul’s conversion. Paul makes mention of this three times in the book of Acts and in the list of witnesses to the resurrection in 1 Corinthian 15.

Paul also mentions how Jesus spoke to him in a vision after he had fallen into a trance, Acts 18 and 22:17. In Acts 23 Luke mentions how Jesus stood by Paul in the night to comfort him because of his persecutors in Jerusalem, and to inform him that he would be going to Rome.

There is an element of mystery whether Jesus, now in a body can be in more than one place at one time. Before His resurrection He could not be in Galilee and Jerusalem at the same time but whether Jesus’ resurrected body is capable of this we do not know.

4. *Why are there not more reported physical encounters with Jesus during revivals?*

When I began to research such encounters one of the first places I looked were the great revivals of church history. There are many fascinating accounts of God's presence, supernatural manifestations and even angelic ministry but I was surprised how few there were of actual visual, physical encounters with Jesus.

It seems that during such seasons of God's blessing the manifest presence of God is so strong that such physical encounters are not needed because God is making Himself so real in many other ways.

5. *Why is Jesus sometimes described in dazzling glory and at other times in a more ordinary appearance?*

Just as angels can reveal different degrees of glory so can Jesus. Sometimes angels are seen as awesome beings of light and at other times they can appear and not be recognised as supernatural. We are told in Hebrews 13:3, *"Do not forget to entertain strangers, for by so doing some people have entertained angels without knowing it."*

In the encounters in this book there are times when Jesus appears as He is in His heavenly glory and at other times He reveals Himself in how He must have looked when He was on the earth.

What is certain is that no one has seen Him in all His magnificent majesty. The closest is the Apostle John on the Isle of Patmos. One day, when we have new bodies, we will be able to see Him as He is and we will be like Him, 1 John 3:2.

References

Introduction
John White, *Putting the Soul back into Psychology*, p87

Chapter 1 Fred Lemon
Breakout, Marshall Morgan Scott © 1977

Chapter 2 Doreen Irving
From Witchcraft to Christ

Chapter 3 Chris Lambrianou
Escape from the Kray Madness. Pan Books, © 1995

Chapter 4 Sundar Singh
Sadhu Sundar Singh, Cyril J. Davey, STL Books, © 1950

Chapter 5 Moussa
"From Works to Grace" Moussa Koné, Testimony of an Imam's Son

Chapter 6 Fred Wertheim
Jews for Jesus web site, used with permission.

Chapter 7 Ram Bali Singh Personally shared with the author
Sheik Mohamid Amin *Miracles among Muslims* – Darg – p 88, 89
Paul Ciniraj Used with permission

Chapter 8 Ernie Holland
Hooked by Ernie Holland

Chapter 9 Gulshan Esther
The Torn Veil, Gulshan Esther, as told to Thelma Sangster Zondervan, Copyright 1984, latest edition 2004

Chapter 10 Smith Wigglesworth
Ever Increasing Faith Chapter 5 & p 121, Stanley Frodsham, *Smith Wigglesworth, Apostle of Faith,* Gospel Publishing House, 1948, pp 13 & 58–59.

Chapter 11 Betty Baxter
http://www.geocities.com/bettybaxterstory/index2.html

Chapter 12 Miracles of Healing
Amelia *I Believe in Miracles* by Kathryn Kuhlman, Marshall Morgan Scott © 1962

Barry Dyck *Visions of Jesus,* Phillip H Wiebe p74, Oxford University press, © 1977

John Occhipinti Ibid p 76

Chapter 13 Johannes Facius
God Can do it Without Me, Sovereign World © 1990.

Chapter 14 We Both Saw Jesus
Visions of Jesus, Phillip H Wiebe p77, Oxford University press, © 1977

Chapter 15 Richard Wurmbrand
Tortured for Christ, Wurmbrand, Richard, Living Sacrifice Books, © 1976

Chapter 16 Samuel Doctorian
And Then I saw Him Samuel Doctorian © 2000, Published by Bible Land Mission Pasadena, California, USA Pages 61-70, 89-97.

Chapter 17
Gul Masih Gul Masih, letter written in Urdu from Sargodha Jail, March 8 1993, Quoted in *Secrets to Spiritual Success*, Paul Estabrooks, Sovereign World 1996, P79

Oswaldo Magdangal Oswaldo Magdangal, *Arrested In The Kingdom* (Witney, Oxon, UK: Open Doors UK1993, p221 *Secrets to Spiritual Success*

Chapter 18 Brother Yun
The Heavenly Man, Paul Hathaway © 2002 Monarch Books Pages -,34-51, 251-261

Chapter 19 Norman Campbell
Sounds From Heaven, Colin and Mary Peckham, Christian Focus ©2004, page 107

Chapter 20 Yonggi Cho
Dream Your Way to Success, Neil Kennedy, Logos International, © 1980, pages 119-121, 156-158.

Chapter 21 Dan Baumann
Imprisoned in Iran, YWAM publishing, © 2000.

Chapter 22 Stephen Jeffreys
Seven Pentecostal Pioneers, Colin Whittaker, Marshall © 1983

Chapter 23 Jesus in Arabia
Miracles among Muslims, Christine Darg, Destiny Image, © 2006

Chapter 24 California and China
California *Visions of Jesus*, Phillip H Wiebe p77, Oxford University press, © 1977
China *Christianity Today*, Karen Feaver, May 16, 1994, p33,34

Chapter 25 Choo Thomas
Heaven is So Real by Choo Thomas, © 2003.

Chapter 26 Mommy I Saw Jesus
Adapted from *Kids Life*: *The Magazine for West Alabama Parents* (May/June 2001), © 2001 Amy Buettner. Used by permission. Copyright © 2002 by the author or *Christianity Today International/Today's Christian magazine* (formerly *Christian Reader). Today's Christian,* November/December 2002, Vol. 40, No. 6, Page 68

Chapter 27 Jesus in the Midst

1. *Picture and story of Jesus in the storm,* Buzz Magazine, In 1987, "Buzz" magazine changed its name to "21st Century Christian." Some time later it merged with "Today" (a magazine which had previously been called "Crusade") - and they together were called "Alpha." With subsequent changes of ownership, the magazine "Alpha" then became "Christianity" and finally "Christianity + Renewal."

APPENDIX 1 Discernment, Dennis Hensley, *Pulpit Helps,* Mar 1996. Page 8

APPENDIX 2 Visions and Dreams, *Miracles Among Muslims,* Christine Darg, Destiny Image, © 2006. *Islam Faithful "See Jesus" After Ramadan,* The 700 Club CBN

APPENDIX 4

1. *The Life of Anthony and the Letter to Marcellinus* p34 -36
2. *Dialogues 4.51*
3. *Luther's Works Vol 6 p329*
4. *Commentary on Acts* 16:10, 9:10, 27:23, 23:11, 7:31.
5. *A Dictionary of Miracles* by E C Brewer Dictionary, P325
6. *A Dictionary of Miracles* by E C Brewer Dictionary, P20
7. *Paul Molinari, Julian of Norwich, P63, 76.*
8. *A Dictionary of Miracles* by E C Brewer Dictionary, P297
9. *A Dictionary of Miracles* by E C Brewer Dictionary, P416

10 *A Dictionary of Miracles* by E C Brewer Dictionary, P416

11 *Walsh Apparitions and Shrines,* Vol 1, p249

APPENDIX 6

1. *Luther's Works* Vol 6 p329.

2007
Postscript

In chapter 15 on page 137 I spoke about a good friend who was in hospital and had just heard he had inoperable cancer and given three to twelve months to live. The wonderful news is that there is now no sign of any cancer and his strength is increasing daily.

2020
Postscript

The above postscript was when the book was first published in 2007. In this revised edition I can report that my friend has made a full recovery and is presently serving the Lord in ministry in New Zealand.